The
Best Little
Boy in the
World

The Best Little Boy in the World

JOHN REID

BALLANTINE BOOKS • NEW YORK

Copyright © 1973, 1976 by John Reid

All rights reserved under International and Pan-American Copyright Conventions. Published in the United States by Ballantine Books, a division of Random House, Inc., New York, and distributed in Canada by Random House of Canada Limited, Toronto. Originally published by G. P. Putnam's Sons, New York, 1973.

All selections from the rock opera *Tommy* by The Who, copyrighted © 1969 by Fabulous Music Ltd. Reprinted with permission of Track Music, Inc. All rights reserved. Reproduction prohibited.

Library of Congress Catalog Card Number: 92-90410

ISBN 0-345-38176-9

Cover design by James R. Harris
Cover photograph by Jill LeVine

Manufactured in the United States of America

First Ballantine Books Edition: May 1977
Fifteen Printings
First Ballantine Books Trade Edition: June 1993

10 9 8 7 6 5 4

This is a book about owning up to one's true identity, yet I have disguised the characters and signed it with a pen name. The characters are disguised to protect their privacy, which I have no right to invade. Using a pen name, though I would rather not, is the least I can do for my parents, who have done a great deal for me. Ideally, of course, it would not be necessary. But, then again, ideally there would be no reason to write a book like this at all.

**The
Best Little
Boy in the
World**

CHAPTER 1

I was eighteen years old when I learned to fart. You may think it's easy for me to write a disgusting thing like that. It's not. If someone had told me on that occasion seven years ago—well, of course, no one was around at the time, I would never have done it in anything but the strict-est privacy—but if someone *had* told me that seven years later I would write a book which began that way . . . the point is, you have no idea how far I've come in seven years.

But this will only make sense if I begin at the beginning.

I am wearing a sheet with a hole cut out for my head and holes for my arms. I am carrying a shopping bag that was empty when my mother gave it to me. It has some bite-size Tootsie Rolls in it now, and some white-yellow-orange waxy candies, too. I am not sure what is going on. It seems naughty, and it's past my bedtime, but Mrs. Connell is driving the car, so how can it be naughty? I am the last one into the station wagon this time. She lifts the gate of the wagon, checks to see that no fingers get caught as she shuts it, but she does not put up the back window. We always put up the back window of our station wagon when anyone is in the

3

back, but Mrs. Connell doesn't want to put it up and down every time we stop.

I wonder whether I am allowed to eat any of the Tootsie Rolls. They haven't said, so I'd better not. The car starts forward; I fall out the back window onto the dirt road, thunk, in the darkness, alone. I am not the kind of little boy likely to be missed in a car with a dozen screaming children. I don't scream.

I am lying on my back on the dirt road, dazed, beginning to wonder what I am supposed to do, beginning to wonder what they will do to me, if they find me, for doing such a bad thing.

I see the car stop up the road. Another ghost has seen me fall out the back window and has passed the word up to Mrs. Connell. Mrs. Connell backs the car up slowly. I am sitting up now, dirt on my sheet, dirt on my hands and in my hair. I am not supposed to be so dirty.

It doesn't occur to me to move from the middle of the road. I assume that Mrs. Connell won't run me over. She doesn't. She checks me all over to make sure I am all right, puts me back in the car, and rolls up the window.

I hope she won't tell my parents.

I am in the hall closet, behind the winter coats, stifling hot, but this is the price you pay to win at hide-and-seek. We don't often have enough children around to play hide-and-seek, but when we do, I usually hide here. Someone may open the closet door and look inside, but I just hold my breath behind all those coats, and even if they thrash around the coats, they never find me. It is pitch black with no light fixture inside and poor lighting outside. Only when the television is on is there any light in the closet, and that is because the television is set in the wall, with the back in the closet and the front in the den. I like watching TV backwards, through a crack in the grating behind the picture tube. Today the television is not on. What am I thinking about there in the dark, my open eyes as good as shut?

I am five years old. I am the best little boy in the world, told so day after day. The worst thing I have done to date is to consider—just to consider—ripping off the mattress tag that says DO NOT REMOVE THIS TAG Under Penalty of Law. At five, the best little boy in the world can read that, but somewhere he has heard the unique *zrzrzrzippp* that ripping off this appendage makes. It's a louder sound than such a small, soft piece of material deserves to make, and so of particular interest.

I would love to *zrzrzrzippp* that stupid tag right off; it just invites mischief, hanging there as it does. What good does it do, anyway? It's our mattress, isn't it? It is incon*ceiv*able that policemen or judges would ever enter the house of the best little boy in the world, whose parents are, by implication, the best—*Wait!* Maybe they would enter to go after my big brother! Maybe I can *zrzrzrzippp* the tag off *his* mattress, and they will come and get *him*—but that is too much to hope for. And when the Law comes and looks down at me and asks—just a matter of routine questioning, mind you, not grounded in any particular suspicion—"DO YOU KNOW ANYTHING ABOUT THIS?"—I will immediately break down and confess. The BLBITW can bring himself secretly to consider ripping off a stupid tag, but he cannot consider lying.

■

Five years old. My father is painting the front door of our early American house in Brewster, New York. We go there every weekend, a million miles from anyone else anywhere near my age, except my brother, nine, who alternately terrorizes and ignores me. Being ignored, of course, is the worse of the two.

My father and I are painting the front door. That is, he paints; I am there to run errands. I am never allowed to paint or saw or hammer. I ask my mother what I should do—I'm bored. "Go help your father." He lets me run errands, which I hate. Or, "Go help your mother." She lets me set the table, which I hate. My brother *loves* to set the table, to make me look bad.

The only other member of my family is Sam, the Airedale, who has rough, kinky hair, which I don't like, and who is about as big as I am. That's something my brother and I fight about: whose turn it is to feed the dog. Poor Sam. We take the frozen leaves and the ice out of his black metal pot, too large and hardware-storish to be called a bowl, and spoon out some cold corned-beef-hashlike stuff from the can. I don't know how Sam puts up with it day after day.

Father is painting the door white. Sam and I are watching, standing on the lawn in front of the house. Father goes off to the barn to get something—it must be too high for me to reach or too much fun or something—and I wander around the flagstone path from the driveway looking for ants to squoosh. (No one has ever told me not to do that.)

Father returns, and he is *mad*. I take my father very seriously, as I suppose most five-year-olds do, and if he is mad, I am scared.

But what have I done? The ants? The mattress-tag thoughts, somehow overheard? He points to the lawn, which now has white splotches all over it. *I* didn't do that! Honest! Nonetheless, I feel guilty. I always feel guilty. I break guiltometers.

"It wasn't that way when I went to the barn. Who else did it if not you?" he asks. True, there is not another little boy for miles, and the evidence is unmistakable. I am being framed.

I didn't do it, I persist. That gets him considerably madder. Now we are talking not about mischief, but about honesty. And if there is one thing . . .

My defense department computer should be calculating the probability-weighted payoffs of alternative courses of action along my decision tree, considering sunk and relevant costs, and determining the only rational course of action: Admit guilt and be done with it. Only F. Lee Bailey could advise a plea of not guilty. However, as I am five, I don't know anything about computers or decision trees, and F. Lee Bailey is still in law school dreaming of the publicity that will come from winning impossible cases like mine. Okay, Dad; I did it. I'm sorry.

Are you *kidding*? No *way*! I have an absolute sense of right and wrong, and I am *not* going to lie, no matter what the consequences, particularly when lying means admitting that I did something *wrong*, for heaven's sake, and jeopardizing my status as the best little boy in the world.

I DIDN'T DO IT! I am screaming now. Tears will appear shortly.

Come in the house. Mother comes to watch. She usually rescues me. (I don't mean to exaggerate: Spankings are as far as it ever goes, and they are rare—of course, I rarely do anything to warrant a spanking.) But honesty is a lesson she feels I must learn.

There we are: I suspended over the ottoman, backside up, yelling that I didn't do it, honest; Father whacking me and telling me in his strongest language—"FOR CRYING OUT LOUD" is his ultimate profanity—that the paint means nothing, but lying to your parents, for crying out loud, is intolerable; Mother thinking to herself how much more it hurts them than me and preparing for the reconciliation. I don't know where my brother is. Probably working on the Sunday *Times* crossword puzzle, or setting the table. Sam is absent also.

I go crying, howling, wracked with the injustice of it all, suddenly tuned in to mankind's suffering through the ages, stumbling, stamping, stomping to my room.

Somewhere beneath the tears I am still a smart, self-centered little kid, and I half realize, anyway, that I am playing this thing for all it's worth. Still, this *is* the kind of injustice and frustration I have heretofore experienced only at the hands of my enormous nine-year-old brother, "Goliath." That the *Supreme Court* should suddenly turn against me—the Court upon which the legitimacy of my standing as the best little boy in the world depends (Goliath is the best little bit bigger boy in the world, in case you are wondering how they get around *that*)—well. . . . My mouth is full of the pillowcase I have been gnawing. I can say no more.

There is a knock at the door. LEAVE ME ALONE! Let me suffer, you who do not even trust your son. My parents are knocking on the door. They have Sam with them. Sam's tail is white. I hear through my emotional straitjacket that Sam got his tail into the can of white paint and accidentally did all the splotching himself. "Forgive us." *HAH!*

■

I remember very little of my first five years, though I keep trying.

How old was I when I pulled the drawers out of my father's dresser, each one not quite as far as the last, like steps, and climbed to the top? My mother came in, instantly terrified that I might fall off. I felt perfectly safe up there, but she set me on the carpet and told me that we never did things like that. And how old was I sometime later when, despite the warning I had gotten on top of Daddy's dresser, I climbed to the top of our bookshelves, leaned the wrong way, and brought the whole thing crashing down, books all over the floor—unhurt myself, but terrified at the sentence I expected from the Supreme Court? (It was commuted.)

I remember standing in Brewster on a hot summer day, bored, watching my mother planting pansies, with all their surprising colors, kaleidoscopic, you never know what combination to expect. What other flower is as unpredictable? I mean, standing there was very boring, but if it had to be some kind of flower, I am glad it was pansies.

We had an elderly black maid, a "Negro" then, of course, whom we loved dearly. She would come up to our room in the country—Goliath and I shared a room—and tickle our feet to make us go to sleep. I don't remember her reasoning, but we loved it, went wild over it, would not go to sleep without it. (No hidden meaning here, really; all she did was tickle our feet.) To this day I am ticklish, but have become considerably less so over the past few years. People are not assigned ticklishness the way pansies are assigned colors: Ticklishness has something to do with where your head is.

I remember sitting in front of my mother's night table with a pencil in my hand and some paper and her telling me it didn't matter which hand I used to hold the pencil, I should use whichever one felt more comfortable. I tried each a couple of times and chose my left one. I don't remember whether I had learned the difference between left and right. Both hands looked alike. Wouldn't my left hand become my right hand when I turned around?

I remember riding around my room in the city, in our West Side apartment, on a tricycle, just around and around in a circle on the orange Howdy-Doody linoleum floor, thinking I can't remember what, fantasizing I can't remember what. Most of the time just bored.

I remember my brother and me being mugged in the park by a ten-year-old, the neighborhood Bad Boy, who I vaguely remember had once been charged with setting fire to the playground with his magnifying glass on a sunny day. He wanted our scooter, and he wanted to bully my brother—which didn't make me feel as good as I would have thought it would.

As there is no particular thrill in bullying a five-year-old when a nine-year-old is available, the mugger said I could beat it. I ran to the edge of the park—our building was right across the street—but I had never, never in my life crossed a street by myself. When I got older they would let me, maybe. Still, my brother was being mugged in the park by a convicted arsonist, and even I knew the thing to do was to run home for help.

There was a woman at the corner waiting for the light to change—we *never* talked to strangers—and I decided to take drastic action. I asked her if she would walk me across the street. She looked at me a little surprised, not very sympathetic—what's there to walking across the street, for Christ's sake? When the light's green, walk. So I just followed her (it wasn't that hard after all, but it felt *different*, all of a sudden being responsible for myself) and buzzed the buzzer of our apartment, fearing the worst, feeling very guilty. How could I explain the loss of Goliath? How could I explain being back here alone? I mean, *How did I get across the street?* My mother quickly grasped the situation through my mumbling and went to retrieve my brother from the ten-year-old mugger, scooter and all.

Shortly thereafter we moved to the East Side.

I remember missing the school bus to kindergarten one morning and my father taking me in a cab on his way to work. He knew the block my school was on, but not the proper entrance. I remember not knowing, either. I had been going for months, of course, but had always found my classroom by following the head in front of me.

Another time, one afternoon in the first grade, they changed school bus drivers on me. The rookie driver asked me where I lived. Where I *lived*? Are you *joking*? I know how to read, I know how to multiply—do I know where I *live*? I live at *home*, that's all. *You're* the school bus driver, not me, for crying out loud—what do you think this is, a *taxicab*? Of course, I didn't say any of that. I just began to well up with embarrassment, which was quickly overtaken by fear—lost among thousands of look-alike buildings, millions of *strangers*—on my own at the age of six. After some thought, I remembered my last name. (Well, I went to the kind of school where everyone was called by his first name and treated very carefully. We were gifted children, you know.) My last name was all the driver needed, apparently, as things quickly returned to normal.

And then another time—I may even have been seven or eight by now, or nine—one of the people who came periodically to measure our IQs and to interpret our ink blots asked me what my religion was. Oh for crying out loud, here we go again. When I reddened, she tried to help, listing off the possibilities. I was on the spot and just took a guess. I sat there kind of expecting her to tell me whether I was right or wrong, as normally happened when I answered a question in school—but this time *I* was the original source. (I was wrong, as a matter of fact.)

Of course, through all these shining performances I was feeling less than entirely adequate. Embarrassed? Look, let me tell you about embarrassment! But it was more than that: It was the basic understanding—that sick, guilty feeling in the deepest recesses of my psyche—that I was a phony. I was *not* the best little boy in the world as my parents thought. I mean, the BLBITW couldn't possibly be so OUT OF IT! I was superpolite, maybe, but not superbright as I was supposed to be. What kind of idiot doesn't even know his own *religion*? I was sure everyone else in the class knew. Chip Morgan certainly knew. He knew what was coming off, believe me. Chip Morgan was wearing white bucks and playing spin the bottle before I had ever *heard* of either one, for crying out loud.

And if I was superpolite, it was for the wrong reasons. I was not polite because I loved other people or was considerate or believed in the Golden Rule, or any of that other crap. I was a goody-goody because it was the proven road to reward. It was the way to play the game. I was one very Establishment little kid. And deep down, I knew I wasn't "good" at all—just selfish, just out for myself. I was a phony, and I knew it.

Meanwhile, the religion thing went even further. If I didn't know my own religion, do you suppose that could mean that I didn't believe in God? Aged seven, and already a heretic. With one simple question the researcher had discovered the evil lurking within me.

There really was evil lurking within me. I didn't want there to be. I didn't ask for it. But it was there. For example, I always forgot the words to the Pledge of Allegiance and to the Anointeth-My-Head-With-Oil psalm that we did at the beginning of school every day. And while I made the best show of mouthing the words that I could, deep down I knew that I was the only one in the class who *didn't understand* what the things *meant*, even, let alone believe that the Lord was my shepherd. *"Anointeth"?*

But while I was dumb, I was not so dumb as to let on just how dumb I was. You never caught *me* asking what "anointeth" meant. Or, later, "masturbate."

CHAPTER 2

I learned to masturbate the same year I learned to fart. Eighteen. I was a sophomore in college. I had been to Europe twice, had won most of the academic honors at my high school and six varsity letters. But I had not learned to fart. Or to masturbate.

I had never farted because I knew it was a bad thing to do. The family would drive to Brewster every Friday evening, and back on Sundays, eating the peanut-butter-and-ketchup sandwiches my mother had made and listening to *Our Miss Brooks*, whenever we could catch it on the radio, or, mainly, fighting. That is, my brother and I would be fighting in the back seat—DON'T CROSS THAT LINE!— and my father would be for crying out loud in the front, wondering how he could be responsible for such brats, while my mother would be predicting imminent 60-mile-an-hour gory disaster if we didn't behave ourselves and let our poor father concentrate on his driving, during all of which I would be getting clobbered, physically and psychologically, by my brother's intimidations—which I probably invited out of excruciating boredom—when all of a sudden the tables would turn. GOLIATH! The car hushed. We all knew instantly, without a word spoken—it is bad enough to *do* it,

let alone speak of it—GOLIATH! ROLL DOWN YOUR
WINDOW! I would already have rolled down mine, hand to
my throat, looking as nauseated as possible, playing my
brother's lapse in manners for all it was worth, again . . .
gasping for fresh air, but really basking in my undisputed su-
premacy: The BLBITW would *never* do a disgusting thing
like that. Here was a level on which I, at little more than
half his age and not much more than half his weight, could
compete and *win* time after time. For some reason it took
him years to learn control, and by the time he finally had,
and we could make it all the way from Brewster to the East
Side without so much as a single—GOLIATH! ROLL
DOWN YOUR WINDOW!—he was about ready to go off
to college. Which left me, naturally, the undisputed best little boy around.

Though sibling rivalry had a lot to do with my hermeti-
cally sealed anus, there was more to it than that. Once when
I was very young, three or four, I would guess, I was sitting
comfortably in my little wicker-weave itty-bitty chair, contemplating the Howdy-Doody linoleum floor of my room,
or whatever, when I was called to the dinner table. We
had company that evening. I sat in my grown-up silver-silk
upholstered dining-room chair—and it felt prickly-
uncomfortable, as though I were sitting bare bottom on a
pile of hay. Now that was funny, because if anything, this
cushioned chair should have been *more* comfortable than my
wicker-weave chair—and I made a number of remarks on
that very discrepancy.

My mother said I could go get the other chair, and followed me into my room, whereupon she lowered my little-
boy-in-corduroy pants and—well, I was *amazed*! I had no
idea I had done that. Mother took care of it quickly, without

a word—but I was mortified. I could think of nothing so vile as what I had done—it was Goliath's laughable sin IN THREE DIMENSIONS, yet, and I determined to be very careful from then on. Another slip like that and the BLBITW could just throw in the towel, for crying out loud.

Some time later, around the age of twelve, at sleep-away camp, I deduced the meaning of the word "fart," though it was too disgusting a word ever to pass from *my* lips. At the same time, I fairly quickly learned that "f—k you" was the single worst thing in the world that could be said by or to anyone, even though on rare occasions of rage, when I really wanted to shock and terrify my fellow campers, in the heat of some truly embittered dispute, I *could* bring myself to come out with it in a stage whisper. Of course, *that* utterance was possible only because I hadn't the faintest idea what it meant. Nor was I about to ask anyone. *I* was no fool, aged twelve. Aged fourteen. Aged sixteen. Around sixteen I suppose I learned what it meant. (And I learned how irrational, illogical, impossible, therefore, was the accepted response—I'LL BET YOU'D LIKE TO—when spoken by one boy to another.) But having some intellectual knowledge of the word's clinical definition was different from my intimate, olfactory understanding of that *other*, unspeakably disgusting word.

Now, after all that buildup, I can't honestly tell you that I remember the occasion of my first deflation. I do remember, in general terms, a period of a few months around my sophomore year in college when, having once given just the tiniest, most hesitating, little-by-little testing sort of vent to what must have been extraordinary pressure farther than usual from the nearest men's room—on a geological field trip perhaps?—having thus once experimented and found, *mirabile dictu*, that I could relieve myself in one dimension without going 3-D, I began gradually to become bolder and bolder and in less than a year I had it down to a science.

Of course, I only did it in private—*never* where there was even the remotest chance that—BLBITW! ROLL DOWN YOUR WINDOW! And to this day, as I still struggle to get out the word, I stand forever in awe of my high school classmates who would *actively seek an audience* while they rolled back on their shoulders, lit a match, and made like some kind of perverted tapered-chinos dragon.

But if the exact occasion and circumstances of my first gaseous relief escape me, I could write a 1,000-page monograph on the occasion of my first masturbation.

I did it by accident, actually; without even using my— look, Ma!—hands. And I'll tell you, I was one happy eighteen-year-old boy. The orgasm—the famous, fantastic, unforgettable, hold-it-back-with-every-muscle-and-nerve-in-your-body (well, I thought-I-would-be-wetting-my-bed, which-at-eighteen-would-have-been-awful) first orgasm— was a degree of six-feet-off-the-ground ecstasy and relief you experience only once. Yes. This was no eleven-year-old's first dribble. I had been saving this, maturing, building the tensions FOR YEARS! So, yes, the orgasm itself was A-double-plus-WOW. But that was really insignificant in light of the larger fact: I had done it! I COULD DO IT! I was the last one in the world to learn how, but I DID IT! After recovering from my initial amazement and emotional exhaustion, I started to do it again. Within three weeks of constant practice I had learned: (a) to do it lying on my back, using my hands; (b) not to do it more than once a night.

But I have really gotten ahead of myself because, as I say,

the remarkable thing wasn't the orgasm itself, but why it had taken me so long to have one.

Let me dispel one hypothesis immediately. I was *not* one of those children who were taught from the first hint of puberty that masturbation was evil, that my thing would fall off if I did it, that my mind would turn to cornflakes, or that my knees would break out in goobers. You should be embarrassed for even having considered such a hypothesis. In *my* family, one of the things we *never* talked about was that thing down there. Never. As it was the only part of the body we never talked about, as we always kept it covered, and as society just manages to ingrain in every child, without necessarily ever getting explicit, this was a Bad Area. This was an area the BLBITW used for one thing, in private, and one thing only.

So I had no old wives' tales keeping me pent up. It was only a matter of learning how to do it.

Now I imagine many children learn as I did, by accident. Only they stumble sooner. I can't give an airtight explanation for how I managed to keep my footing so long, but I can offer some guesses.

Foremost must be the situation just described. It was simply no-man's-land. I would no sooner have fooled around with my Bad Area than I would have stuck my finger up my Other Bad Area. In addition, at some point I learned the phrase—I don't know where I heard it, probably counselors in camp—DON'T PLAY WITH YOURSELF. Well, that just confirmed what the BLBITW already knew. He had not yet developed the kind of fine legal mind that could make the distinction between playing with yourself on the Fifth Avenue bus and playing with yourself in bed.

Then there was the general gut feeling that perhaps

things were not all right and proper down there. And sure enough, around the age of thirteen—by which time I had become very uncomfortable with the whole subject of that area, its uses, its abuses—I noticed that the left side of my scrotum was bigger than the right side. And while I tried as hard as I could not to think about it, I was aware deep down that something was out of kilter. Not in my mind, you understand—I haven't gotten to that yet. A real, gen-u-ine physical defect.

I could think of no way to avoid my annual medical checkup, and sure enough, even before he said "cough," the doctor noticed. Okay, Doctor: Notice it, if you must, but for God's sake, ignore it the way I do. . . . PLEASE don't give it any sort of recognition.

He did far worse than that. He asked me why I hadn't called him when I first noticed it.

Let me give you a moment to let the full force of that mortal blow sink in.

Right? *Why hadn't I told anybody?* Wouldn't that have been the natural, normal, BLBITW thing to do? I mean, are you *hiding* something? ARE YOU HIDING SOMETHING? What's been going *on* down there *anyway?* Hmmmm, you little phony? You're not the BLBITW they think you are, now are you?

Hiding something? Friends, I was hiding everything. But I will get to that.

My defense department computer, defective as usual, should have gone ticking along the perimeter of its linear program and stopped with a buzz and a print-out at the optimal solution: Tell a casual, convincing lie: "Gee, Doc, it only got this way a couple of weeks ago, and it hasn't hurt or anything, so since I knew I'd be seeing you today, I just didn't bother to do anything. I hope that's okay?" That's what Chip Morgan would have said, isn't it?

But me? I said the only thing I could think of—nothing—assuming that sooner or later he would start talking again.

He did, explaining that I had a rather routine "varicocele"—too much blood pumped to the scrotum, which swells it up on the left side and looks a little ugly—but about 10 percent of the male population has it and, unless it begins to bother me, nothing need be done about it. He would call my parents just to let them know.

MY PARENTS? Are you out of your mind? What about the confidential relationship between doctor and patient? I could have you disbarred for telling my parents! Instead, of course, I just let the film wash over my eyes and did a half-hearted Jackie Gleason hamina-hamina-hamina. To my credit, I did not pass out.

I even made it home. And when my dad asked to see what the doctor had called about—to see it—I looked so adolescent-embarrassed that he didn't push it. He may have been the BLBITW, to a lesser extent, in his day, too, which may be why we never talked about these things.

After that experience with the doctor, my Bad Area was unquestionably, more than ever, off limits. I just didn't want to think about it.

So where was I going to learn to jerk off? When was Famous Artists Schools going to start advertising a correspondence course on the subway panels? I might have learned from the birds and bees lecture, but as I say, it was not my father's favorite topic. He made a concerted effort once and got as far as wet dreams and ejaculations—but I finally prevailed upon him to stop. I couldn't take it. Listening would have been admitting I didn't already know it all, which would have seriously called into question my adolescent normality—everybody knew that stuff—and the last thing I wanted to do was to call into question my adolescent normality. I mustered one of my rare performances: Oh, Dad! For heaven's sake (which was somehow in an altogether different category from For Crying Out Loud)—*I know all those things.*

So I didn't learn to masturbate from him. Even if I had let him continue, I doubt the prescribed text included a chapter on that subject.

Well, what about Goliath, for crying out loud? What are older brothers for? It never occurred to me at the time even to wonder whether he had mastered this art—as I say, I did my best to keep my mind off such subjects—but I found out last year, when we finally got to know each other, that indeed he had been doing it since he was twelve—sometimes right in the next bed from me. Gad.

In fact, it dawned on me after our recent conversation, as I sifted my early years over and over . . . that night in the East Side apartment—oh, WOW, of *course!*—there was that night when he kept wiggling his toes against the sheets ever so softly—just loud enough to get on my nerves to keep me awake—and then we started fighting, and I went in to my parents' bedroom to complain—at which he took more than the usual offense, for some reason—but kept wiggling his toes all the same when I returned—my *God!*

So I would have had an apt instructor in Goliath, but we didn't have that kind of relationship. Sure, we loved each other. We were *supposed* to love each other, remember, so I certainly did. But ours was not your all-American Wally-Leave-It-To-Beaver kind of fraternity.

I first went away to overnight camp when I was ten. Goliath was in his third or fourth year at that camp, and a moderate big shot. He knew the tent ropes. I, on the other hand, was only now being cast onto my own resources for the first time and was, as usual, terrified.

Everything was going smoothly until I arrived at my tent and met my counselor, an ex-marine. He told me to make my bed. Fine. I unlocked my trunk, which was miraculously in my tent when I arrived, took out the sheets and such, and began to make the bed.

"Don't forget the rubber mattress cover," the marine said.

"The rubber mattress cover?"

"Yeah. The rubber mattress cover."

I searched diligently for it, though I had never heard of one before and could not remember its being on the list of things—thirty-two white Camp Winnepesaukee handkerchiefs, fourteen pairs white Camp Winnepesaukee athletic socks, one athletic supporter (optional to age thirteen)—we had packed in Brewster, the last time I saw the trunk. I searched knowing I would not find it, that I had failed miserably, that I would be sent home by the next available train, a disgrace to the family. That phony feeling again.

"I don't think I have one. Could I make the bed with this cloth one?"

"You're supposed to have a rubber one. It says here that you wet your bed."

THAT I WHAT? Oh my God, I think he's talking about *that area*! We *never* talk about that area. The last thing I was prepared to do was to talk back to an authority figure, let alone an ex-marine, for crying out loud, but this was the white paint on the lawn all over again. "No, sir, I don't wet my bed." Now, the fact is that maybe once or twice in my life, like any kid, I had wet my bed. But what's going on? Authority figures don't make mistakes. Maybe my parents hadn't had the heart to tell me that I wet my bed and sent me away to have this marine tell me. Have I told a lie—do I really wet my bed? A lie to a *stranger*, no less? But I am ten now, not five—you can see how far I've come—and I am almost certain that I don't wet my bed, that there is some mistake.

We went back and forth a couple of times—"No, I don't." "It says here you do, but I'll cure you of it soon enough." "AGH!"—when Goliath happened along. For perhaps the first time in my life I was overjoyed to see Goliath.

I got Goliath to admit his blood relationship with me, and then, oh-so-relieved, I asked him to tell the ex-marine that I did not wet my bed. If anyone knows, it should be you who sleep in the same room with me! F. Lee Bailey couldn't have constructed a stronger defense.

"How should *I* know whether you wet your bed?" That is all Goliath said. He went off to play tennis.

So I wouldn't have learned how to do it from my brother.

I can think of only four possible courses of instruction that remained, three of which I can eliminate out of hand. I could have *read* how to do it somewhere, but the BLBITW didn't start reading dirty books until a couple of years ago. I could have learned from our sex education program in school, but all they told us about was good posture, deodorant, and taking your hat off indoors. I could have learned about it "in the street," but the street in Brewster was a state highway on which I was not allowed to ride my bicycle, and the street on the East Side was populated primarily by doormen.

That leaves the general category of friends: in camp, in high school—freshman year in *college*, for crying out loud.

Camp was quite an awakening for me. All of a sudden I had to fend for myself, and the standards by which performance was measured were largely physical rather than academic. Unfair! They are changing ground rules on the BLBITW, who has never even learned to play baseball (how can you play baseball if the only other kid within miles—we had thousand-acre zoning, I think—is always setting the table?)—baseball, the national pastime, the symbol of all that is normal and wholesome.

Having become quite used to being one of the best in my class at whatever I did (multiplication, state capitals), I couldn't bear the embarrassment of standing out there in right field, left out, frightened to death that someone, some stupid lefty crackerjack batter, just *might* slam one out to right field. And there I would be, trembling, knees weak, CHOKING—and miss it. *Everything* is a self-fulfilling prophecy, my fielding being no exception. Invariably, once a game, somebody had to hit a ball out there; invariably, I would miss it. So I only played when I had to, one game a year.

My dreaded once a year in right field, as any former camper will have guessed, was during color war. *Every*body had to play. And the last year I played, I must have been about fourteen, my worst nightmare came true.

Sure, I must have missed the inevitable right-field fly—that was so routine I can't even remember it now. But someone up there, the Great Phonifier, had something far more humiliating in mind for the BLBITW. It was "the bottom of the ninth," in our seven-inning game, with our side one run down, the bases loaded, two outs, and a three-and-two count. (I *swear* I am not exaggerating.) Need I tell you who the three-and-two count was *on*?

I'll give you a hint. It wasn't Goliath. Nor was it Tommy Roth, the camp charisma, the fifteen-year-old whose friendship and respect I sought in every way I could. Tommy was on the *other* team. And now, at fourteen, while I was hardly the camp charisma, I had become a color-war force to be reckoned with. I won all my swimming events, I led the relay, I won my tennis match on a 16–14 set, I shot a 94 on my ten-bull. But while Tommy was doing all these things in *his* age group, he was also leading the team sports. Like baseball.

Tommy had come down to watch this game, with most of the rest of the camp, because the five color-war points that rested on it were becoming increasingly important to the outcome of the entire war. Tommy, of course, had not said a word to me for the past four days—this was war, after all—and was now a few yards away, laughing at me, and at how I was going to CHOKE! CHOKE! and blow the whole thing. HEY, ADAM'S APPLE! *CHOKE!*

Meanwhile, of course, my team captain—not the baseball team captain, mind you, though he was there, too—the *color-war* captain, and the *head coach*, for crying out loud, were telling me to take it easy: The poor pitcher was under tremendous pressure, was going to CHOKE!, and all I had to do was watch the ball closely and only swing on the off-chance that it came anywhere near the plate. A walk with the bases loaded would tie the score, and our big guns were up right behind me. WALK'S AS GOOD AS A HIT!, HEY, PITCH—CHOKE!, FLY'S DOWN, PITCH!, WALK'S AS GOOD AS A HIT!

The pitcher, who, sure enough, was choking his brains

out too, let fly with a ball that, while headed more or less in my direction, promised to sail several feet over my head. Possibly over the backstop. As it came, all I could hear was Tommy: HEY, ADAM'S APPLE, *CHOKE!*

If I hadn't swung at that fucking little ball, it might have been the pitcher who would be writing this book now.

So in camp I was kind of a loner. I was good at the solo sports and developed a menacingly good build, at least by the standards of kids whose parents can afford to send them to $1,000-a-season summer camps. I was smarter than my peers, I never got into any trouble. . . . I was respected, maybe even feared a little bit—but not exactly loved or accepted.

I *wanted* to be accepted, no question about that. But I couldn't bring myself to do the standard acceptance-winning things. An acceptance-winning thing in camp would be anything that annoyed the counselors and made me one of the boys. And if whatever mischief I made were of sufficient quality to broach the possibility that I might be *sent home*—to me, the ultimate unthinkable disgrace—then I might even assume a leadership role among my peers. I had all the other characteristics. However, the BLBITW simply could not bring himself to any sort of mischief. He had been molded too well. Much as he wanted acceptance from his peers, he would not risk losing it with the authorities or—God forbid—risk being sent home.

Thus I was on fairly good terms with many of my fellow campers, but not intimate. I *certainly* could not reveal that I didn't know how to masturbate. Through the songs ("You ought to see me on the short strokes. It was so grand, I used my hand," sung to the tune of "Finiculi, Finicula") and through snatches of conversation, I began to learn the word and its synonyms. I would hear thirteen-year-olds bragging about how they could do it in ten strokes—but I never really knew for sure what it meant.

High school was much the same: I was respected, I had some friends, but evenings I was home writing extra-credit reports to keep me on my throne and get-me-into-the-college-of-my-choice, and weekends I was up in Brewster, no longer bored, writing extra-credit reports.

I heard enough to know that everybody did it; I couldn't risk asking anyone what or how. That couldn't be the way you find out, anyway, for crying out loud! You don't get hair to grow down there by *asking* someone how—it just happens. It is part of adolescence and puberty. Can you imagine the ridicule if I admitted that masturbation hadn't happened to me yet? WHAT ARE YOU, ANYWAY, SOME KIND OF HO-MO?

So I didn't ask any of my friends in high school either. I just kept wishing it would happen, yet knowing deep down that things were out of kilter down there—the varicocele, and all. . . .

There was one instance that might have been taken as an encouraging sign, around the age of thirteen, that, had it not been for one integral aspect, might have buoyed my self-confidence markedly. At home on the East Side one night, I had a wet dream. Not that I knew the term for it or made any connections.

I remember that it took me some time to decide for a certainty that I hadn't just wet my bed, that there was a difference, that there was nothing to be em*bar*rassed about, that this was one of the things I had been *wait*ing for. Nor did I tell anyone about it. Actually, my wet dream left me quite upset. So upset that—zoologists, Guinness, Ripley take note—it is the last one I had.

I had apparently repressed all future wet dreams, though I didn't know it at the time. I just began to assume, when there were no repeat performances, that things were rotting away down there. And under the circumstances, I felt that was maybe all for the best.

I'll tell you this, though: I was one energetic teenager. Talk about repressed sexual energy! I swam a mile before classes, won all the academic honors, swam miles after classes, ran cross country, wrestled, played soccer, did untold millions of sit-ups, headed the lab assistants, wrote for the yearbook, edited the newspaper (respected, mind you, not loved like the class president), and wrote extra-credit reports until they were coming out of every teacher's ears. One such in the eighth grade had the unimposing title "A History of the Balance of Power in Europe, 476 A.D. to 1053 A.D.," which I managed to cover in about fifty pages, plus maps.

And then I got to Yale and shared a room with Roger Ritter, a young man not unlike Tommy Roth, who, although not necessarily destined to graduate with high honors, really knew where it was at. Roger had fallen in and out of love a hundred times. He spent the first week, while I was reading the orientation materials, driving around to Vassar and Barnard and Wheaton. He was forever asking me to excuse him and his date for a few hours while they used the room; and those evenings when he hadn't used the room, he would wiggle his toes against the sheets, ever so softly, the way my brother used to do.

Only he must have had a slightly different technique, as

every morning when I woke up there would be a Kleenex next to his bed. By Thanksgiving of our freshman year I had made a remarkable deduction.

I was confirmed in my suspicion when Roger started asking me why there was never any Kleenex at the foot of *my* bed in the morning—particularly, I suppose, because I never asked him to let me borrow the room. Well, I was just your typical attractive-but-shy Yale freshman, perfectly healthy, just a little naïve.

Luckily, I remembered hearing one of the counselors in camp state that wet dreams were by far the more mature alternative to beating off. So, by the age of seventeen, having begun to debug many of the flaws in my defense department computer program, I simply answered that I did beat off a couple of times a week, that I preferred to do it on evenings when he had not yet come in or was already asleep, that I didn't happen to use the same Kleenex-by-the-side-of-the-bed choreography, and—the clincher—that actually I preferred to have wet dreams. He was impressed, and I avoided yet another chance to learn how to beat off.

Though I had bluffed Roger, his prodding had been enough to get me to make an all-out effort for normality. I forced myself to remember clues from an awful story I had heard in camp:

The way it works, see, you get a dozen guys in a cabin for a round-pound, see, with the lights off, see, and you offer a banana split to the guy who shoots first, right? Well, you let everybody but Joey in on it. Then you turn off the lights, see, and start slapping your wrist with the first two fingers of your other hand, like this—thap, thap, thap—and pretty soon Joey starts panting and shouts that he's won, see, so you turn on the lights, and you're *all dressed, going thap, thap, thap against your wrist, and he's sitting there all messy, looking like an* idiot!

And one night, in private of course, and halfheartedly, I guess you'd say, and certainly not fantasizing anything sexy—just waiting for it to happen, but not really expecting that it would—I started thap, thap, thapping down there, Kleenex at the ready just in case. Ten, twenty, maybe thirty thaps, and nothing had happened. I remembered my fellow campers bragging about how it only took them ten strokes, so after a few more, rotting away down there for sure, just as I had suspected, and simply not wanting to think about it, I quit and went to sleep, feeling sorry for myself.

When I say feeling sorry for myself, I do not mean depressed. That was entirely another feeling. I enjoyed being depressed. I would spend hours being depressed, walking around thinking cosmic martyr thoughts about the great burden I was carrying and about the delicious irony of the best little boy in the world's being so bad, after all—but, as only the best little boy in the world could, bearing all the pain himself and sparing his loving parents. And so on.

I did spend hours like this, wondering whatever would become of me, how I would cope—fantasizing stunning confessionals that would shock the *New York Times* into omitting the Sunday edition and causing me to be sanctified in my own lifetime, or maybe only after being burned at the camp totem pole—pondering suicide—all these juicy thoughts which even I realized were not really so terribly painful. I would never have admitted it, I suppose, but being a martyr was kind of fun.

But when I really got down to brass tacks—when I was in the shower and I looked down at that varicocele or thought I saw others looking; when my group was assigned to baseball for the afternoon; when form demanded that I get a date for the senior prom or Dr. Whatshisface wondered why I hadn't told anybody about this—then I felt real pain, I felt sick inside, I desperately wanted help I couldn't ask for—and I felt sorry for myself.

Anyway, my freshman roommate reminded me that every kid in the world did it, but he didn't show me how.

Imagine my surprise, therefore, my ecstasy, my relief, that evening of my sophomore year in college, in a room all to myself, part of a three-man suite—a room so small that I had suspended my bed like the Brooklyn Bridge between a six-foot wardrobe closet on the left and a six-foot book-case on the right—when squirming around on my stomach and thinking thoughts I doubt I can bring myself to describe . . . and squirming some more, and then beginning to feel almost as though I could not stop squirming even if I had wanted to, and wanting to stop squirming, and trying to hold it back just as I had repressed my wet dreams, trying desperately to hold it back, because it was *so bad*, and squirming so noisily on Brooklyn Bridge that my defense department computer was sending desperate signals through my fantasies that one of my roommates might be attracted by the noise, so YOU'D BETTER STOP, you idiot, HOLD IT BACK, you . . . *Ahh*hhhhhhhhhhhhhhhhhhhhhhhhhhhhhhhhhhhhh. . . .

That great event occurred shortly before we went on Christmas vacation. I was bursting to tell someone. I had begun to develop some close friends—friends I felt I could even trust, to a point. But to tell this would have been too much. It would have completely wrecked my image as a fairly "with it," impressive young man. However I phrased it, the listeners would have heard: "Last night I learned to do for the first time what everyone else in the world has been doing from the age of eleven." And if they asked me—not out of cruelty, it's just the logical question—WHAT TOOK SO LONG? (read: What's *wrong* with you? WHAT ARE YOU HIDING?). . . .

Then we came back from vacation, and I was in talking with my roommate and closest friend, Hank, whom I admired no end, who was so *cool*, who knew just what to do at all times, who was so good-looking, who could play *baseball*, for crying out loud—and Hank told me: "I saw a lot of my friends from high school when I was home and—well, you just wouldn't believe what they're doing now. Do you know what they're *doing*?" He asked this with a mixture of incredulity and disgust. I didn't know for sure, but I made a sickeningly good mental guess. "They're masturbating," he said.

My ego ideal was so disgusted by the whole idea, he went on to tell me—as easily and unself-consciously as if he had been talking about the crummy food in the dining hall—that *he* had *never* masturbated. (How could he admit that?) Hank said he thought it was gross and perverted. He said real sex or wet dreams were far more healthy.

"*Mas*turbating?" I echoed him. "Oh, that's disgusting." Indeed, I was as amazed and sickened by his revelation as he was, only for different reasons.

Thank God I hadn't told him! Or anyone! Apparently, I realized, a few degenerates at camp did it (you know about those summer camps); my freshman roommate did it (he had indeed, I recalled, spent several years in a summer camp). But that was about it. Nobody cool did it. Nobody decent did it. The lights were on, and I was the messy idiot.

▪

And one final thing. I can't put it off any longer. I should really have mentioned it several pages back where I was talking about how that isolated wet dream was, well, a mixed blessing, never repeated. My wet dream was about Tommy Roth.

CHAPTER 3

All right, so you had a wet dream about another boy. Is that what knotted up your adolescence so badly? Look. The famous statistic is that one out of three males reaches orgasm with another male at least once in his lifetime. That's from Kinsey. So relax. You didn't even have physical sex with him, did you? You just dreamed about him, right?

RIGHT! Oh, RIGHT! I swear to you that I am desperately trying to keep this wicker-weave throne, to live up to the image all the authority figures have of me. RIGHT! Even if I had wanted to play out my—wait, strike that— even *though* I wanted to play out my fantasies—even though I *longed* to play out my fantasies—I would never, never have done so. And as a result, no one will ever find out that I have such fantasies. I'm clean, Officer. You've got nothing on me.

But now that we are on the subject, Officer, I can tell you a thing or two. I happen to know that some of the kids at camp were doing more than just fantasizing. Please don't say I told you, but there was a lot of experimenting going on. And with some of the counselors, I think they weren't just experimenting even, if you know what I mean.

Yes, I was only vaguely aware of it as I became an older

camper—like the time Tommy and that counselor kicked everyone out of their tent and closed the flaps on a sunny day—but I was aware enough not to let any of those counselors give *me* back rubs. I was particularly cold to that one who couldn't take his eyes off my body. I was so disgusted by the thought that this ugly man wanted to touch me, it made me shiver.

But, oh, what I would have given to be Tommy's real best friend. God, how I wanted to be *like* him, to do the same mischievous, self-assured things he did, to have muscles and blond hair and a smile like his. Nothing in our relationship would be disgusting, nothing unmentionable. Just to be like the Hardy Boys, two blood brothers, two cowboys . . . that's it: two cowboys.

In elementary school I had felt the same way about Chip Morgan. We would go up to his apartment after school and eat Oreos and watch TV, or play knock hockey, or play that board game called Baseball, where hitting and fielding are determined by a spin of the plastic spinner. Or Chip would put on his swim trunks and bathrobe, like Joe Palooka, and we would mess around with his boxing gloves, or wrestle, like we used to watch on Channel 9. Then his mother saw him that way once, in his trunks and bathrobe—well, I guess it was underpants, not swim trunks—and got angry and said never to dress like that again. But I was eight, nine, ten those years and too young to know what was going on. I just liked it.

I was going through what they call a stage, right? I was *supposed to* hate little girls when I was a little boy. I was *supposed to* hate those dance lessons we were all forced to take, aged ten, those multiplication dances where my ego required that I be chosen at any early round in the progression, while at the same time I was praying madly that if the progression caught me at all, it would be for the last round only so I would have to go bumbling around the floor just once, and then only while everyone else was too busy dancing, and maybe trying to sneak a feel, to have time to watch me bumble. Everyone else, of course, had things well under control, like that pitcher in color war.

I was going through a stage. Sure enough, young boys all knew: One of these days a little hair would start to grow in odd places (it did); the clerk would stop calling you "Miss" when you phoned in a grocery order (he did); muscles would begin to bulge all over your body (they did); and those little girls you had been ignoring would begin to drive you wild. I was waiting for those girls to start driving me wild, but I was very skeptical.

I was all of eleven when I first "knew" what I was, in a tentative, semiconscious sort of way, hoping to be proved wrong, but knowing for certain, down deep, that it was snake eyes for keeps. No fingers crossed.

My parents were having a party in Brewster: mostly businessmen, a few doctors and a few lawyers, some real estate types, their wives—the standard grown-up dinner party. Sports jackets and slacks: pipes, cigars, and cigarette smoke; the hubbub cresting, hushing momentarily, then rushing to crest with even greater force.

I was watching *Superman* in the den. My father passed through with one of his guests. He was saying something like: "I've read that, too; but ten percent just couldn't be right. There couldn't be that many people with homosexual tendencies. . . ." Something like that. Frankly, I am surprised I do not remember the exact words, because the incident itself I will never forget. That is all there was to it. They passed by; I sat there with my head aimed at the TV—but my face on fire with recognition. I *knew*, I'm not sure how, but I *knew* I was in that 10 percent. So *that's* the word for hating dancing school, for not playing baseball, for admiring Chip's athletic prowess, for the phony feelings, and lonely feelings, I sometimes felt.

It was hazy and vague, aged eleven. But I had gone off to camp the previous summer, and I was about to enter junior high school: I was being jolted into thinking a little, into becoming aware of myself. I no longer just looked at the picture of the Golden Gloves boxer in the magazine and liked it—I started to wonder *why* I liked it. And whether I was supposed to like it. And if not, whether I would stop liking it.

By the age of thirteen I was poignantly aware of what I was. But my inner shell of defense was impregnable. I had found out about myself, but no one else would ever find out as long as I lived. That stigma and keeping it a secret were the fundamental core of my mind, from which all other thoughts and actions flowed.

I would somehow cope. I would somehow enjoy hour after hour of cosmic depression, day after day, year after year. I knew what was happening now, and I spent most of my time writing programs for my defense department computer. You would never catch *me* spilling the beans in my sleep. You would never catch *me* electing art instead of science, playing Hamlet instead of tennis.

One ingenious defense was to remain as ignorant as possible on the subject of homosexuality. The less I knew, I reasoned, the less chance that I would start looking like one or acting like one. I *wasn't* one, damn it! Those people I saw on the streets with their pocketbooks and their swish and their pink hair—they disgusted me at least as much as they disgusted everyone else, probably more. I would sooner have slept with a girl, God forbid, than with one of those horrible people. Do you understand? I wasn't a homosexual; I just desperately wanted to be cowboys with Chip or with Tommy.

So I never read anything about homosexuality. No one would ever catch *me* at the "Ho" drawer of the New York Public Library Card Catalog. Bachelor J. Edgar Hoover and his lifelong friend Clyde Tolson would have to be a lot more clever than that to trip me up.

All I knew about it was that it was awful. You could pick this up from the one-liners that fellow campers and classmates threw around or from occasional references in books or even the newspapers. But the most coherent explanation I had was from my father. One of his favorite stories between my ages of twelve and fifteen or so—my formative years, he thought, though I think he was about ten or twelve years too late—was about how *his* father had heard a rumor that one of my father's teachers was a homosexual, so when my father came home from school, his father asked him whether that man was indeed one of his teachers, and my father said yes, and his father beat the living daylights out of my father, who at the time it happened was always about the same age I was when the story was being told. Have you got all that? The two morals were unmistakable: I should be eternally grateful that my father was not the unreasonable tyrant that his father was. And homosexuals are the scum of the earth.

That was the extent of the knowledge about homosexuality I allowed to penetrate my defenses.

Another important line of defense, the most important on a practical day-to-day basis, was my prodigious list of activities. "Highly motivated; a self-starter," the teachers would write on my character reports. Hell, yes, I was motivated! No one could expect me to be out dating on Saturday nights if the school paper was going to be on the stands on Tuesday. No one could expect me to be partying over Christmas vacation when I had a list of seventeen urgent projects to complete—I would be lucky to find time to open my presents, let alone go to parties or date, for crying out loud.

And who do I know who gives parties in Brewster? That, of course, is where we went each weekend and holiday, which was a line of defense all its own. For all my classmates knew, I spent Saturday nights whoring it up in Brewster.

Really, it was not awfully hard to fake my way through high school. High school was more talk than action. At least my kind of all-boys high school was. And I did my best to learn to talk, or at least listen, as though I were just like anybody else. The better-looking, more outgoing kids *were* dating and partying; but nobody's parents were paying all that tuition to have their sons turned down by the college of their choice, and I was far from being the only one chained to a desk on Saturday night. Who would know that my chains were self-imposed?

I went to just enough parties to remain credible, though not enough to learn all the new dances, notably the twist, for the rapid demise of which I prayed religiously. The relationship between dancing and sex was all but inescapable.

Sex got me nervous; dancing made me self-conscious. And I have since learned that it takes only one thing to dance creditably: self-confidence. The twist lingered for years and was a continual source of embarrassment. You can't *do* it? Really? *Why not?* Well, Doctor, you see those thousands of people out there on the dance floor? They're all normal, Doctor. The guys are going nuts over the girls; the girls are going nuts over the guys. But me, well, I just can't tell you why I can't do the twist, Doctor, but it would make your hair stand on end if I did. Just let me suffer.

Of course, I tried to avoid doctors and would no more have considered talking to a psychiatrist than one of the ten most wanted criminals would consider stopping to get directions from a cop.

The closest thing to a shrink we had in school was a math teacher named Sir who doubled as the guidance counselor. Sir took psychology courses at Princeton every summer and liked to play heavy little mind games with his students. He was married and had kids, so he couldn't be accused of anything.

Sir had developed one of his heavy relationships with me—twisting my words, insisting I must be hiding things when I wasn't (Well, I was, of course, but those were other things and surely none of his business), talking about love-hate relationships, for crying out loud, when all he was supposed to be was adviser to the student newspaper. That was our official connection, through the newspaper, and he was telling me I hated him. I didn't—although I began to when he kept insisting I did—you see! You *do* hate me! Now *why?* What's really on your mind?

What was really on my mind was that he only did this kind of thing with the best-looking boys in the school, and the same ones I liked—so if it takes one to know one, *maybe he was on to me.* Perhaps I hadn't hidden everything as well as I had wanted. That suspicion caused me to be all the less communicative. Why aren't you *communicating* with me, young man?

One day I had to deliver something to him just before class. Usually, this would have been routine: Weave your way through twenty noisy kids; excuse me, Sir; a handed note; exit. I handed him the note and turned to leave. DID I TELL YOU YOU COULD GO? Sir had been in the Navy and was a stickler for manners.

"I'm sorry, Sir," I said, standing about a yard from him.

"Come here," he said. I inched a little closer, hoping not too many of the students were watching all this.

"Come *here!*" he demanded, so I inched some more— what the hell, did he want me sitting in his lap, for crying out loud? As I was inching, he started to reach out to grab my wrist, as he would occasionally do—no big thing; teachers grab students' wrists sometimes when they are talking to them—but I . . . instinctively . . . jumped back. WHY DID YOU BACK AWAY?

I didn't know why I had backed away. And if I had known, I am sure I could never have articulated it there in front of the class. I muttered something about its just having been a reaction—nothing intended, and I was sorry. A RE-ACTION! You see! You see how much worse that is? That proves that subconsciously you are afraid of me, that shows that subconsciously . . .

Subconscious, hey? Well, we were indeed nearing Secret City. But he could delay the start of class no longer, and our stage-whispered exchange was tabled. He was on to me. I avoided him for the rest of the year.

Close as Sir came, neither he nor anyone else ever penetrated my defenses. The guns of Navarone were like water pistols in a shoe box compared to the fortress that guarded my secret.

Short of doing myself in, which, like every adolescent, I enjoyed contemplating from time to time, my last line of defense was to turn and run. I only had to resort to it once. I was sixteen, researching one of my extra-credit reports at the Museum of Natural History. On satellites, I think it was. I was examining the Explorer capsule that was on display, watching the continuous film strip that simulated its flight through space, looking at the plastic astronauts cramped in the cockpit, when a man next to me asked some question about the capsule. I hadn't noticed him before. He was unassuming: average height, maybe twenty-five, slim, wearing a gray windbreaker zipped up halfway. Your nondescript man. I answered his questions; he asked a few more. We speculated for a while on what it would be like to be an astronaut—drinking Tang, floating weightless. . . . Then he said: "Now let me show you what interests me."

What interested him was the tropical bird exhibit, dimly lit, birdcalls echoing around the halls—a nice enough exhibit, but evidently of little interest to others. It was deserted. We looked around for a little while, he told me that some of his friends had painted the backgrounds of the exhibits, and I began to wonder how I was going to get away. Mainly I was bored, but I was also beginning to feel uncomfortable with this man. Then I felt his hand DOWN THERE! JESUS CHRIST! No one but the doctor had ever touched me down there. As I pushed his hand away, he was saying, "Would you like a blow job?" I was terrified. Half because I was being molested by some perverted old man (twenty-five), and half because *I didn't know what a blow job was*. The world was caving in again, my inadequacy on display right there in the American Museum of Natural History. I choked out a tortured "No!" as I ran out of the exhibit, out of the museum, and most of the way home. He shouted after me—*shouted* in the hush of the tropical bird exhibit—"How can you be so NAÏVE?—AÏVE? Ïve? ïve?—ve?"

I wonder what made him think I was naïve? I hadn't stopped to *tell* him I didn't know what a blow job was. He must have read it from my behavior. Maybe he figured that anyone who would bolt from anything so pleasurable *had* to be naïve. And of course he had to say something; it must have been an uncomfortable minute for him also.

I was in knots. The experience was so unpleasant, with so many implications and ramifications for me, I couldn't even analyze it clearly, as I had learned to analyze most things. And the worst part was, I *didn't know* what a blow job was. Sure, I had heard the expression, but I never thought I would have to know what it *meant*. *Anointeth?* Surely no teacher would ever put it on a quiz (although in my more paranoid moments I would imagine such quizzes—perhaps given by that guidance counselor). Nor would any classmate ever *ask* me what it meant. In the first place, they all knew already. And if there were, conceivably, anyone left in the world who did *not* know, he would be just as mortified at the thought of asking as I was.

Needless to say, when I got home, I locked myself in the bathroom with the dictionary and read all forty-three definitions and connotations of "blow." Equally needless to say, you can't buy mental health for the price of a dictionary.

Of course, I regained my senses quickly, thankful that no one would ever find out what had happened. In fact, I quickly turned the incident to my advantage—psychological judo: The next summer in camp I told the story, more or less as it had happened. I related my genuine disgust. I heaped all the worst invectives I could on that perverted *thing*, to establish my own normality—and I even managed to deduce from the subsequent conversation what the hell a blow job *was*.

My counselor at that time was Jack Simmons from the University of Pennsylvania basketball team. He would frequently joke about my muscular calves, with what I thought just might be more than casual interest. Jack told me I had overreacted to that situation in the Museum of Natural History. He told me he let females *or* males suck his dick because it felt good. ("So that's what it is!") Hadn't I ever been blown by a girl? he wanted to know. Sure, I let chicks suck my dick, I told him, but I would never let a *guy* get near it, you could count on that!

Another time, the same year, sixteen, our English class had to go downtown to see the off-Broadway production of *Moby Dick*. We could go when we wanted, with whomever we wanted, so long as we saw it in time for the exam. I somehow contrived to go with Brian Salter, surely the dumbest boy in the class and surely the most attractive. Oh, how I wanted to be cowboys with Brian! He was, of course, the star of the football team (not big and heavy: coordinated), the basketball team, and, yes, the baseball team.

I had managed to become friends with him, despite my good grades and good standing with all the teachers, by drinking. By this time I was able to convince my parents to let me stay alone in the city some weekends ("I could get more work done that way"), and I would either borrow some liquor from our cabinet or drink the liquor Brian's parents had given him (his parents had read a different edition of Dr. Spock) or else go with him to buy some on the street. We couldn't usually pass for eighteen, but we could persuade passers by the liquor store to get it for us. And we would walk up and down Madison Avenue drinking from a paper-bagged pint of some *awful*-tasting scotch, which I detested and loved at the same time.

Anyway, Brian and I went to *Moby Dick* together. I spent most of the performance fantasizing how he and I would become blood brothers and go off to Wyoming—soaking up the cosmic tragedy of its impossibility—and occasionally having to change seats in the theater. It seemed that wherever we sat, someone else would come over to join us and be, well, obnoxious: looking all the time, crossing his legs like a pair of scissors instead of like a doughnut. When we left the theater, two of these effeminate types, immaculately dressed, carrying umbrellas in the midst of a water shortage, followed closely behind us. Brian didn't seem to be particularly bothered by all this. *He* had nothing to hide. I pointed out the menace, and we quickened our pace. They managed to keep up. Dis-*gusting*! I mean, sure, I wanted to be cowboys with Brian in Wyoming, but there was no *telling* what those *queers* wanted.

Adrenaline flowing, I decided to build up some normality points, just in case Brian had ever wondered. I stopped short, turned around, and in the middle of an intersection, as a matter of fact—I shouted that if those two queers didn't stop following us, we would bust their little asses! They flushed, brandished their umbrellas, and fled.

So I was not exactly taking all this lying down. I was working very hard to maintain my cover. *This* double agent was going to keep his lines straight and die a natural death. Perhaps I would instruct the Chase Manhattan Bank to open a sealed letter upon my death and send it to the publishers of the *New York Times*—a letter that would stun the world. What had been planned as a half-column obituary for this upper-level public servant would suddenly become front-page news. Every playwright in the land would strain, and fail, to capture the true agony and magnificence of the burdens I had borne, the brilliance of the ruses I had constructed to throw everyone off the trail. . . .

But until that time, mum's the word.

I somehow managed to keep from getting a hard-on in the showers. And I somehow managed to avoid attacking Brian. Well, only the way cowboys would attack each other on TV, you know—maybe a hard, but basically comradely, fight, which would end up with us both exhausted and even better friends, arms around each other's shoulders for support—he could win if he wanted to; maybe I wanted him to.

I went out for wrestling, but not for the reasons that you might expect. Not consciously, anyway; I swear it. I had been a swimmer during the winter season, but all those miles before classes and miles after classes must have built my stamina to the point where I lost all concept of speed. Year after year, as my stamina improved, my time got worse. When I showed up at the pool after soccer season was over one year, the swimming coach suggested I try wrestling instead.

I was not a terrific wrestler. It takes practice, and while I was strong and had stamina, so did the other, veteran wrestlers. Still, I won my JV matches and then made the varsity when the boy ahead of me got his neck broken. (It was a tough weight class.) Everyone I was scheduled to wrestle turned out to be the team captain or an AAU champ. The coach would huddle with me before I went in there, massage my neck muscles a little (he was married with kids, too), and tell me, "Just try to stay off your back." Sometimes I did manage to keep from being pinned, which meant the other team got only three points, not five, for winning my weight class.

Once, though, I came up against an even match. I was even winning, riding my opponent as I had been taught to in practice, accumulating riding time on the clock, which in the event of an otherwise-tied score would determine the winner of our match, and basically, for the first time, really in control. It was a good feeling, for a change. Perhaps too good. About three-fourths of the way through the match a hot shiver went through my body, and I went limp—my weight still on him. He was too exhausted to take much advantage of the fact that I had, well, lost my wind—and the match was over. I won, but I try not to think about it.

Somehow, as I say, I managed to cope with high school. I had serious doubts about my ability to cope with college. You *have to* date in college. You *have to* know what's coming off. Goliath had already had about eleven passionate affairs in college, which, without any embarrassing details, were top-priority dinner table conversation back home—and the Supreme Court was beginning to send interrogatives my way. They wanted to subpoena one of my girlfriends.

CHAPTER 4

In high school it had been enough to learn to check out attractive girls on the street—look them up and down, leer a little, nudge my companion (naturally I only bothered with this nonsense when there was someone else around), maybe sigh or pant a little, or mutter something dirty—and then go back to noticing the boys.

Noticing attractive girls was not as easy to learn as it sounds. There was no department in my subconscious responsible for spotting pretty girls out of the corners of my eyes, as there was in the subconsciouses of my friends. I had to remind myself consciously of my friends. I had to remind myself consciously to look or else suffer the embarrassment of being reminded by a friend's poke to *catch those legs—oooo WEEEEE!* But I ran a significant risk in leering and nudging: As I was attracted by boys, not girls, I had to use the most mechanical techniques in deciding which girls were "attractive." (If I knew instinctively, I was afraid to trust my instincts.) While others would have a simple groin reaction, I would nervously rush through a little checklist. I knew girls in laced shoes or combat boots were out. I knew legs were important and had heard someone talk scornfully about a girl with "piano legs," so I tried to avoid those. I

49

would ignore any girls whose heads did not at least come up even with the parking meters as they walked by, as well as those whose heads brushed the bus stop signs. Frizzy redheads, for some reason, were out. Girls who looked like boys except with ponytails were out. The hardest part, especially under winter coats, was to determine whether a girl was "built" or just fat. There was nothing whatever to be gained by leering and chortling over a dog. One slip like that and my cover would be blown: *You're not really attracted to girls!* YOU'RE FAKING IT!

My back-up defense in such situations was myopia. I purposely kept my glasses off—they weren't very strong anyway—so that any omitted or mistaken leers and nudges could be blamed on my ophthalmologist.

In college you had to do more than just leer and chortle. You had to date. Maybe you didn't have to if you were ugly, and maybe you didn't have to if you weren't worried about your normality. But if you were me, you had to date.

Not counting high school parties and camp dances, where everyone had to go by the busload—more like holding a special dancing lesson than a date—I can remember having had three dates prior to entering Yale.

The first was when I was seven. It was with Holly Frye, who would cry at the slightest provocation. She was unbelievable. She would cry if the teacher squeaked chalk against the blackboard. She would cry if cookie crumbs got on her dress. She would cry when she heard someone else crying. I certainly didn't like her, but for some reason I found her one afternoon with my mother and her mother in our car, picked up from school, on the way to my room, of all places.

It was a disaster. We started playing with my chemistry set, the litmus paper bit, and she used an entire piece of my litmus paper to test—I don't know what it was, probably some lemon juice or something of equal scientific significance. Well, any fool knows you are only supposed to use just a tiny corner of the litmus paper! The whole piece! My God, she used the whole piece! I didn't hit her. I just said something nasty and then ignored her. Which was hard to do, as she immediately began to wail and cry and scream and howl and was finally taken home, much to my relief.

Dumb girl. Ukh.

My second date, I think I was fourteen or fifteen. I can't remember this girl's name, but I remember that she was a regular at the dances I would force myself to go to. She had a four-inch chin, but was otherwise attractive for a fourteen-year-old girl, as best I could tell. Maybe she would grow into that chin, or have a chin job. Meantime, when she walked through doors, she had to turn her head sideways so her hand would reach the door knob before her chin hit the door. I didn't care. I was infatuated at the time with a genuine preppie, who flew into the city only for vacations and who suggested we double. My eagerness to be cowboys with this preppie knowing no bounds, I got a date.

We doubled to a double feature, my first movie date. Movie people are forever making movies of kids going to movies early in their sexual careers to experiment with arms around their dates, around a little farther, hand cupped around what will someday be a breast, another hand moving toward the popcorn in her lap—and the movies the four of us went to may well have been movies like that. I can't recall. I just spent the four hours watching what the preppie did and doing as much of it to my date as I could bring myself to do. That is, I put my arm around the back of her chair. And once, by mistake (I had long since lost all feeling in and control over that arm), I think I brushed her shoulder. Maybe it was the back of her chair. Maybe it was her chin.

The problem was, I felt nearly as uncomfortable *not* doing anything to her as I would have felt doing something. I wanted to do something, the way the preppie did, but all I could do for four hours was wonder what it was that made me different—an upside-down chromosome? The Great Phonifier? What was I going to do when it came time to get married?

We took a cab back uptown—in the days when the meter started at a quarter and clicked by nickels. Had I tried to kiss my date good-night, which of course could not have been further from my mind, her chin would probably have gored my Adam's apple.

My third date was also when I was about fifteen, my last summer in camp, and Tommy Roth's. Tommy was dating a counselor at our sister camp. Who was I dating? I had to be dating somebody, so I was dating Hilda Goldbaum, from Queens. Hilda's chin was in proper proportion to the rest of her face and body, which in total couldn't have weighed thirty pounds more than mine. She was particularly weighed down by two of the most enormous, terrifying boobs I could imagine. But that's how things happened to pair up the first night they took a busload of us seniors out to the sister camp for a dance, so it was Hilda and me for the summer.

Brother-sister camp dances, as you may know, are very risky affairs that send camp directors' hearts aflutter. Once, in 1932, a girl got pregnant possibly as a result of one of these dances, and the sister camp went out of business then and there. Since 1932, the state militia had been called out to guard the exits at all of our brother-sister camp dances, and the only way you could possibly hold your head up in the bus on the way back to camp was if you had been *missed*—that is, if you and your girl had been missed at some point during the course of the evening. Maximum points were scored by the couple who could turn up under the yellow circle of flashlight—down at the rifle range. Where they have mattresses.

"This bus ain't leavin' till we find Tommy. And when we *do* find him, he's gonna catch hell, lemme tellya."

Five minutes later Tommy and Kathy are discovered down at the rifle range. The bus pulls off with all kinds of adulation being showered on Tommy. Hey, Tommy! What were you shooting down there anyway? Har, har, har. The camp director would find out about it the next morning, telephone Tommy's parents, and threaten to have Tommy sent home. Tommy's proud father, who had been caught down on the same rifle range in his day, would mention Tommy's three younger brothers, nearing camp age at $1,000 apiece—and the matter would be dropped.

So Hilda and I *had* to be missed. Yet this was one test of my manhood I was just going to have to fail. I couldn't bring myself to seduce Hilda into the dark piney woods. I would just have to blame it on the security guards and change the subject when people asked me.

As it happened, Hilda had different ideas. She led me through a maze of piled tables and chairs, through the kitchen and the dishwashing apparatus, to an unguarded ratty old warped sinful-looking screen door, and out into the dark piney woods. She was hot, she said, why not go for a walk? I stopped after a few yards to try to marshal my resources for some kind of brilliant excuse. When I got older I planned to use the one about having had my thing shot off in the war, but Hilda, I knew, would not have accepted this from a fifteen-year-old. Maybe I could say it was shot off at the archery range. I started to open my mouth, in a hesitating sort of way because I was not sure of what I would say, and Hilda grabbed me as though she were an alcoholic and I were the last bottle left on earth. She pressed her lips hard against mine. I gritted my teeth and held my breath.

It was awful. The kiss itself, my first on the lips, could have been worse. It was just like pressing your lips against something squishy. Nothing more, nothing less. But knowing that it was nothing more, when it should have been, and, far worse, knowing that when this kiss was over (it was dragging on and on), Hilda and the world would have discovered that I didn't know how to kiss—that was awful.

Finally she loosened her grip and moved her face away, and I prepared for the worst. I had just stood there, after all. Whatever kissing is, however they do it in the movies, I had just stood there. My major achievement had been to repress the natural impulse I had to wrinkle up my nose. But do you know what she said? She said, "Oooow, that was *wonn*derful. It's been a *month* since I had a man!" That line sent me a lot of conflicting signals. Of course, I was tremendously relieved to know I could pass for a lover just by standing in the woods letting her squish her lips against mine. I felt like remarking in amazement, crying with relief, laughing at the ridiculous thing she had said, gloating at having pulled it off. And now she was doing it again.

I had heard of French kissing, but I didn't think we were doing it. Before she decided to get into *that*, I figured I would take a gamble, newly self-confident as I was, and when she backed away, I said in my deepest, most leadership kind of voice, "I think we'd better get back before they miss us." Apparently, I noted, she had gotten her rocks off, as she dutifully followed her man back to the dance.

The following week, Hilda and Kathy somehow contrived to get over to our camp to see Tommy and me. Tommy was delighted, and after lunch (I remember it was ravioli) he commandeered an empty tent for us. He put the flaps down. I kept trying to protest about the grave risk we were taking, but Tommy had had the flaps down before. He started making out with Kathy, lying on top of her, kissing her, putting his hands all over her. I made some very awkward attempts, with more help from Hilda than I wanted, to do roughly the same things, hoping against hope that some counselor would come along and break it up. Even being sent home would be better than this. And by now, all things considered, it might not have been altogether bad for my image at home to be sent back for this. My parents weren't pushing, but they let me know I would be more than welcome to start bringing girls home, to start dating under proper circumstances, to go to more dances—and who was I planning to take to the Junior Prom?

But no counselor came along. Hilda, meanwhile, was getting ready to go all the way. It was time to French kiss. She pried open my mouth with her crowbar tongue and stuck it in. Agh! *Germs!* Germs, hell: *ravioli!* I don't mean to be vulgar; but her breath smelled like ravioli, and I felt like puking. Or running, or passing out. But there was Tommy, whose respect meant more to me than anything, making out gleefully with Kathy. *Please* stop. *Please* don't look at how awkward I am. *Please* Great Phonifier, at least don't make me puke.

End-of-rest-hour was bugled out over the loudspeaker, which, thank God, was the call for retreat. It was over. The girls had to go back with the counselor who had brought them over. If anything, Tommy thought I was more normal than ever. Kathy was happy. Hilda was happy. I went for a gargle in the lake.

That was the sexual experience I brought with me to Yale. And now I had to date in earnest. I was in the majors. A few people were even thinking about getting *married*, for crying out loud.

Freshman year I rested on the laurels of my fictitious wet dreams and thap, thap, thapping. The first thing I did that year was subscribe to *Playboy*. Like a blind man at a silent movie I would religiously thumb through my monthly *Playboy*, forcing myself to check out, leer, and nudge my roommate, Roger. I liked *Playboy* because I didn't have to worry about chortling over a dog by mistake. I would hang the centerfold on the wall over my bed for all to see. Of course, each time I returned from a vacation, I told my roomie lascivious stories designed to be impossible to check. I was still hung up on a couple of girls at home, I said, and what's there to do in New Haven, anyway? Albertus Magnus High School?

The authorities seemed to be on my side. Freshmen were not allowed cars. Girls were allowed in the rooms from four to six on Tuesdays and Saturdays, or some equally Victorian bits of time. But was I going to argue with prudish administrators?

The people at Yale were genuinely considerate of freshman problems and offered counseling services of all kinds to make it easier to assume manhood, to conform to acceptable social standards. On an *ad hoc* basis, faculty members would also try to help. More than one would look at my cosmic depression expression (I thought it looked cosmic, anyway) and ask me what was troubling me. I remember being alone in the office of a young geology professor who radiated sympathy and understanding as he invited me to open up. He seemed to sense that I had never opened up to anyone; he wanted to help me break out of my shell. Go ahead, he said. He wouldn't be shocked.

The last time someone had told me to go ahead and say the worst thing I could think of, I was eleven, just finishing elementary school, over at Wendy's house for a class party. We were playing a new game. Everyone was given a crayon and a scrap of paper. We had to think of the worst word we could and write it on the paper. Then we would fold the papers, hand them in, and Wendy would read a story— only the story had blanks in it, and every time she came to one, she would fill in the word from the next folded paper. Fun?

No. Like all party games, it made me nervous. Just how bad a word were you supposed to use? I think someone asked that, or maybe several of us did: Wendy made it clear that we were supposed to write a really *bad* word. Well, my natural instinct was to write a word like "darn" or even "damn." That was about as bad as I could usually get. In fact, while "darn" was tolerated in our house, "damn" was not. But I was well aware that normal kids had vocabularies far filthier than that, and if the object of this crazy game was to be bad, I wanted to be bad with the best of them. I had been trained to win, after all. And there may even have been a tinge of rebellion in what I wrote. As the papers were all anonymous, I could do just what they said, and write a really bad word.

Wendy collected all the papers and started reading her story:

Once upon a time there was a young prince named Arthur and a young princess named Guinevere. They lived in a . . . toilet, by a beautiful . . . ugly, on the other side of the hill from a . . . wart.

One day, feeling kind of . . . backside, the prince and the princess called their . . . puke on the . . . devil, and said: "We are going out to take a . . ."

Wendy burst into tears and went running to her mother with what I could only assume was my word. In retrospect I have to congratulate myself not only for having written the worst word, but also for having written the only word that happened to fit the context of the story perfectly. But at the time, I was a nervous wreck. If I didn't look nervous, they wouldn't know it was me who wrote it, but I kept trembling anyway. (Of course, if Chip Morgan had written that word, he would have just sat there smirking mischievously or, if caught, would have taken his spanking and exile without even a gulp. In fact, if Chip had done it, then I would have wished *I* had.)

But I *had* done the deed, and Wendy's mother, who had apparently not sanctioned the game to begin with, came running in to find out who had the red crayon. *The red crayon!* Of course! How could I be so dumb? How could I fall into their trap?

Actually, there were several red crayons, so that, while guilt was clearly written in four letters over my face, a reasonable doubt had to remain in the mind of the jury, and they did not call the Supreme Court. But that was the last time I was going to fall for any of this "Go ahead, tell us your worst thoughts; we won't be shocked!" shit.

I wanted to open up; I just couldn't risk it. In martyr-think, telling one solitary soul breaks the perfect record. If I was going to be lonely, then I was going to be the loneliest boy in the world. Tell one soul, and the shell is broken forever. No turning back. You have lost control of the secret. You have given life to an idea which would otherwise die with you.

The thing about opening up was it had to be to the right person, or what good would it do? I didn't want sympathy from a young geology professor; I didn't want to be given the name of a prominent psychoanalyst; I didn't even want the address of the local gay bar (until my junior or senior year I didn't even know there *were* gay bars). What I wanted was to be cowboys with someone like Brian or Tommy or my freshman roommate with the Kleenex, Roger, and my sophomore roommate without the Kleenex, Hank.

It was obvious to me, in a theoretical, mathematical sort of way, that I could not be the only straight-looking, athletic young man in search of someone to be cowboys with. Yet it was equally obvious to me in a very real, practical sort of way that it would be impossible for me to find the right buddy. Because he, too, would be pretending with all his might; he, too, would refuse back rubs and look girls up and down and leer. Even if one in ten boys really did have "tendencies," who was going to risk everything on a one-in-ten chance?

I guess I was never more tempted to take the one-in-ten chance than with Roger. We shared the same dorm room, beds just a few feet apart. He had gone to a summer camp. And he frequently would laugh and say, "Hey roomie! Wanna jump into bed with me?"

Tempting? But he was kidding. He *had* to be kidding. He laid his girlfriend twice a week in that bed, so he had to be kidding. He was so sure of his masculinity that he could even afford to joke about being queer. Maybe he had doubts about me (no Kleenex) and was trying to trap me. I would accept one of those invitations to bed, he would get nauseated and violent, and then he would call the dean and say he wanted a new roommate because I was a homosexual.

The dean would call me in and ask if it were true. I would deny it. He would hook a machine up to measure my pupil dilation and show me two sets of pornography. At the sight of naked women and pussy and untold other horrors, I would wrinkle my nose and feel like I had a tongue depressor way down my throat, and my pupils, all defenses at my command notwithstanding, simply would not dilate. Then he would show me pictures of young athletes (no doubt from his personal pornography collection, although that wouldn't have occurred to me at the time), and I would force my nose to wrinkle, I would say I thought it was disgusting—but the machine would know. My pupils would be as big as nickels.

Yale would not expel me. They would give me a private room, daily therapy. And they would call my parents for permission for the therapy and send them a letter confirming that their son was a queer.

Sophomore year you got to choose your own roommates for the next three years. Roger and I parted on friendly enough terms (well, friendly enough for him anyway), and I spent the next three years in a three-man suite in one of Yale's several colleges, as the upper-class dorms are known. One of my roommates was captain of the lacrosse team. The other, Hank, was more of an intramural jock, the touch football type, and president of the Yale Key, the group charged with presenting Yale's best face to the public. I was hopelessly in love with both of them, though of course I couldn't let on.

My lacrosse-playing roommate spent most of his time doing just that or else off with the other preppies in his circle, playing pool, watching TV, studying, and, no doubt, feeling superior to all his classmates who hadn't been tapped for the club. I didn't see him very much, and I guess I really didn't love him at all. He just turned me on.

Hank was around much more often, and he and I were truly best of friends. Hank I loved no end.

In writing honestly this way, I don't want to give the wrong impression. Presumably, it rubs you wrong to read about guys loving other guys. Perhaps you instinctively picture me as having been, at best, the assistant-soccer-team-manager type tagging along with the Big Man On Campus, wearing very thick glasses, and getting nose bleeds at the slightest exertion. *Real* guys don't love other guys, right? Perhaps so. But at least to all outward appearances, I was a real guy, and something of a Big Man On Campus myself.

True, where I was good-looking, Hank was downright charismatic. And though I could beat him in tennis and could swim faster, he was clearly the better athlete. But if anything, I spent less time studying than he did, and the little publishing empire I ran was at least as noteworthy as his Yale Key. I even got my face in *Time* once (way in the back, a small picture). So we weren't exactly Wild Bill Hickok and Andy Devine, if you know what I mean. If only I could have told Hank that I loved him.

I didn't want him to love me back. That would probably have ruined it. (Well, that would have made him queer, you see, and who wants to be cowboys with a queer?) As it was, we were simply best friends. We did a lot of stuff together. We helped each other out. And I just had to keep from going overboard. For example, I could buy him more gifts than he bought me, and more expensive ones—but I had to know my limit. I could go far enough that he would react: Hey! Terrific! Thanks! But a hair farther, and he would think to himself: Jesus Christ, what's he *doing*?

Sometimes I would buy him things, because I wanted to, and tell him I had gotten them free, so it wouldn't look bad. I bought four season's tickets to the Yale Playhouse and told him I had gotten them free. So he accepted a pair, and I was guaranteed of doubling with him six times that year. Of course, I would have preferred going just with him, no dates. But I had an image to build. If I had to date, it might as well be to a bunch of plays, where all you have to do is sit and watch—nobody makes out at plays—rather than to dances or parties or drive-ins. In case the girls came back to our suite after one of the plays, I was in no great danger. You will recall that my room was so small I had to suspend the bed like the Brooklyn Bridge over the wardrobe closet and the bookshelves. I had arranged the room this way, and failed to build any kind of ladder, at least in part to keep all but the most vigorous of pole vaulters out of my bed. And I was careful not to date pole vaulters.

I was sneaky, but I had to be. We would frequently go out hunting for a little pussy. (I could never bring myself to talk that way.) Girls always travel in pairs, and, fortunately, the pair is always a beautiful girl and a dog, for obvious ego-boosting reasons. Hank was better-looking than I was, so I would simply say: Oh, wow! Sure, let's make it with those girls! Yeah! I'll take Kathy; you can have Gladys. Hank, of course, would no sooner have gone to bed with Gladys than with the Creature from the Black Lagoon. But, to his ever-lasting credit, he was too considerate of his best friend to say Go Screw, or even to go home with Kathy and leave me to fend for myself.

So, while I am not particularly proud of having aborted so many of Hank's copulations, I always managed to make it home with my image of normality intact.

Almost always. One summer we went to Europe together. (It wasn't Wyoming, but it would serve.) We were in Tossa, on the coast of Spain. The Sangria in Tossa is made the way it is made here; only to each glass they add a jigger of 100-proof brandy and a jigger of 100-proof Cointreau, and then it costs only a quarter a glass. Hank was drunk. The inevitable Kathy and Gladys, British birds this time, came into view, and we spent the customary hour walking around with them, looking for a place to dance, telling them about Yale and about our nifty hotel room. Then, while they went off to the bathroom to reconnoiter, Hank and I went through our little ritual. Wow, those chicks are dynamite! They're dying for it, too! Yeah, let's screw 'em! I think they'll come back with us! Yeah, wow! *"I'll take Kathy, if that's okay with you, Hank."* *"Yeah, okay, what the fuck,"* Hank said, obviously drunk out of his mind, and the world caved in. What a funny way to mete out the death sentence: "Yeah, okay, what the fuck." But that is of course what Hank had done. "How should *I* know whether he wets his bed?" "Why didn't you call me about this when you first noticed it?" "Who has the red crayon?" "Do you want a blow job?" And now this, the worst of all.

The girls came back; my head was awash in adrenaline. Hank asked them if they wanted to come back to the hotel. Sure they did. Hank took Gladys's arm, and Kathy and I followed. Gladys was chewing gum, obviously delighted. Kathy was less than delighted—yes! she would find a way to avoid sleeping with me!—but, while I wasn't Hank, I was apparently, to my dismay, good enough. I was silently going bananas.

Hank and I, of course, were sharing a double hotel room. Not one of those where we slept together in the same double bed, though there had been many of those. (Can you imagine sleeping like that—with Ali MacGraw, if you prefer—and not being able to touch?) This room had two single beds and was ample for the four of us. But whatever was going to happen with Kathy, it simply could not happen in the same room with Hank. I could accept death. I could not accept torture.

I said I liked privacy when I slept with a girl—a little lame, but reasonable, and I knew Hank would prefer privacy, too. It was so late at night the front desk was deserted, so I couldn't rent another room, even if there had been one. I went downstairs to the desk, behind the desk, and stole one of the keys hanging by an empty post box—hoping that it was indeed the key to a vacant room and that no one would be returning even later that night to use it.

The BLBITW actually stole the key. Kathy and I adjourned to the vacant room. I immediately went to the bathroom and locked myself in, water running madly to drown out any thoughts that might otherwise be overheard. Was there any way out? I couldn't think of any. At least Hank wasn't there to see; that was the main thing.

I emerged from the bathroom. Kathy was sitting on the bed. Kathy was no Hilda Goldbaum. She was one attractive girl, as even I could tell, and she was not about to do any of my work for me. But I wasn't really up to it, either.

I'm sure my unhappiness and discomfort showed, and that sort of thing is contagious. I doubt Kathy was much happier than I was. I took off my clothes, except for my shorts, and, as it was two in the morning and no one was helping Kathy take off hers, she had no logical alternative but to take them off herself. We got into bed together. Luckily a fairly wide bed. I put my arm around her, and after a little while I muttered something about being sorry, that it wasn't her, that I was sorry, and I was dead tired, and would she like to go to sleep? Yeah. I turned over on my stomach and lay motionless—as far from sleep as anyone could possibly be, of course—for about three hours until there was a faint suggestion that the sun was on the rise. I rustled enough to wake Kathy and said that since I had stolen the keys to the room, maybe we had better leave before they found us. I would walk her back to her hotel room.

We tiptoed out and back to her hotel. It must have been about five o'clock, judging from the light. I don't know what she was thinking through all this. No doubt she thought I was strange, and no doubt it was not a pleasant experience. Conceivably she thought she wasn't attractive enough to turn me on—well, of course she wasn't, but I don't mean that—and, depending on what little problems *she* brought to the encounter, the evening could have upset her as much as it did me. None of that occurred to me at the time.

I left her and walked at my utmost cosmic to the beach and lay down in the cold sand to wait until it was late enough for me to go back to my legitimate room. It was a nice place to feel depressed, absolutely still except for some stuffed sleeping bags here and there in the distance; an over-turned weatherworn dinghy up on the beach; a little drift-wood; a pale moon growing paler as the sun rose. A nice place to feel depressed, but I was in no mood for that. I was feeling sorry for myself.

I tried to sleep on the beach—I was exhausted—but I couldn't. I just kept thinking. Finally the sun was well up there, perhaps eleven o'clock, but much more likely eight or nine, and I went back to our room. Hank and Gladys were asleep in each other's arms. I lay down on the other bed and kept thinking, waiting for them to wake up. Eventually, hours later, they did. Hank had a slight cold and a hangover; Gladys lit a cigarette. I tried to grin what I thought would look like a satisfied grin and explained that Kathy and I had gone for a walk along the beach and I had taken her back before the hotel people discovered the stolen key. After her cigarette, Gladys went back also.

Hank smiled. I tried to smile. How was it? I asked. "Good, but I think I caught a cold."

"As long as you didn't catch anything else," I managed out of my pretend-normal vocabulary of words and expressions I didn't really understand. He smiled.

"How was it?"

"Good," I said. Best friends don't have to say more than that. They don't have to impress each other or compete with tales of exploits. Hank treated sex as a meaningful thing (even a drunken one-night stand with Gladys)—he didn't masturbate, remember—so neither of us had to go into details about our private experiences. "Good" was enough. Thank God.

Strategically, as with the Museum of Natural History debacle, the whole thing had worked out okay. Hank had virtual proof, short of being an eyewitness, that I screwed girls. Not that he ever thought about it either way, I suppose.

Meanwhile, I was afraid that we might run into Kathy and Gladys again—or that Hank would. Kathy had undoubtedly decided I was queer and had undoubtedly told Gladys. Either Kathy or Gladys would undoubtedly tell Hank. Hank would ask me why I had said, "Good," if I hadn't touched Kathy—and why hadn't I touched Kathy? Then he would leave me the keys to the car, pick up his suitcase, and, sickened by the thought that I had even contrived to sleep in the same double bed with him, rush off to Paris as fast as he could, never to speak to me again.

The hotel people had apparently figured out about the other room. They asked us to pay for it and said they were sorry, but they had no more vacancies, we would have to leave.

Wonderful! Tossa was packed with tourists; all the other

hotels were full, too. We had to leave for Paris that morning, and we never saw Kathy or Gladys again.

When I got back to the States and had to do some heavy normality pretending, I would tell how we were evicted from our hotel in Tossa for raping two English birds.

The dates I had in college were almost always friends of Hank's girlfriends. I had no black book of my own. I got along with them okay. One in particular I saw on and off during a whole year, and she would come to all the mandatory football weekends and college parties. I felt bad about "using" her as a cover, but I needed a cover. Her name was Hillary, and she was Hank's girl's best friend.

She was not unattractive; she was bright, considerate, and, best of all, something of a prude. Just what the doctor ordered. I could make all kinds of advances, trying to get my arm from around her shoulder (a position that I had mastered and that she allowed) over and around her breast. She would never let me touch her there, or down below, which was fine. She could go back to Vassar and tell Hank's girlfriend about my advances; Hank's girlfriend would tell Hank; Hank would think I had normal inclinations, if less than normal success. And if Hank ever asked, I just might suggest that things had gone a little farther than Hillary wanted to admit.

Of course, I began to wonder why Hillary wouldn't let me do anything. Not that I wanted to—just that I wanted to know what was wrong with me. That is, what other people perceived as being wrong. The bad breath syndrome.

It was not bad breath. Once after the play or the postgame party, back at Hillary's hotel room, on the same floor as Hank's girl's room, I got my hand around her shoulder and started moving it across—and Hillary explained that she liked me well enough, but she just couldn't let herself go with me because—get this—she thought I was only interested in her body. *Hah!* I hadn't opened up to her, she said. She didn't know the inner me.

Hank would usually get home from these evenings around three, and for all he knew I had come in only a few minutes earlier. Sometimes I would wait up for him. We frequently had the post-game beer parties in our suite (all the more reason for needing a date), and I would clean things up while I waited. How was it, Hank? "Good." How was it, he would ask. "Good." (If you are wondering why Hank came home at all, as well you might, I have to say, first, that sometimes he didn't, but second, and mainly, try to remember how much different things were just a few years ago. Short hair, no dope, all-male schools, virginity . . . very few years ago.)

Though I managed my way through these evenings with Hillary, I didn't enjoy them at all. I didn't enjoy pretending. It went very much against my superhonest instincts. But I didn't enjoy always getting home before Hank, either. Why did I have to be the social cripple? What were he and my other roommate going to think if I always got home before they did?

One evening I decided it was time for me not to be the first one home. I was walking back from Hillary's hotel. Instead of going back to the dorm, looking first to see that no one was watching me and feeling tremendously guilty—I ducked into another hotel and asked for a room. "No luggage, sir?" "No luggage," I gulped, feeling exposed, guiltier still, but determined. "Then you will have to pay in advance." Twelve dollars.

I went up to the room and tried to sleep, with only moderate success. There was no clock or radio in the room, and no phone. When the sun in the window woke me, Sunday morning, I had no idea what time it was. I waited in bed as long as I could, and then went out into the street—again stealthily to be sure no one saw me. It is unlikely any of my friends would have—it was seven-fifteen.

That's what the clock above the newsstand said. So I walked around feeling guilty for two hours and then went to make my grand unshaven entrance in last night's wrinkled clothes, hoping my roommates might possibly have woken by this time and noticed that my bed was made, and no me anywhere in sight.

Of course, they were asleep, so after turning on the lights in my room for extra effect, I tiptoed back out and walked around for another hour.

At quarter past ten they were still asleep. I hadn't slept much myself and was exhausted by my ridiculous fraud. But I had invested $12 and lots of energy in it and had to have it go as planned. Finally, on my fourth attempt, just before noon, I walked in and saw my roommates were up and reading the Sunday *Times*. I walked past them into my room as nonchalantly as I could, with a simple, "Morning." I waited a minute for the applause, or at least for a question or two. After all, we had been living together for nearly two years, and this was the first time I had ever stayed out all night with a girl. My best friend Hank should have had something to say.

Hank kept reading the paper. I took off my tie and jacket and sat down with them to read the paper. Nothing.

A couple of days later I broke down and asked Hank,

"Hey, didn't you notice that I didn't come home Saturday night?"

"Oh, yeah?" he asked. "How was it?"

"Good."

"Good."

CHAPTER 5

It wasn't a bad life, surrounded by Yale's most attractive, preppie young men. A little frustrating, maybe.

If only I had had someone to talk with. The single most important thing in my life that I thought about for hours each day, that determined what kinds of activities I would participate in, how I would spend my time, who I would sit with at lunch—the most important thing in my life had been kept a total secret for *ten years* now that I was turning twenty-one, about to graduate. (Applause, please.)

Ten years, and I had never once been able to speak honestly, to open up.

That's not a healthy situation.

I was so inhibited and uptight and defensive I couldn't even get stoned. Marijuana had come into its own by my last year at Yale, and two of my best friends, sophomores named Brook and Fred, used to smoke all the time. Not wanting to be left out, I would sometimes smoke with them. I would smoke my head off down in their room, but I would not get stoned.

Not even a buzz. Grass did not turn me on. What did were the occasional playful scraps Brook and I would have, the way college pals do. Brook had wrestled in high school back in Tulsa, I had wrestled in high school, we were both high (he on the dope, I on him)—and we would flex our competitive egos to see who could pin whom. I usually won when Brook was stoned because the grass dulled his competitive spirit. I could never pin Fred, because I could never goad him into action. He would sit in a lotus position on the floor, his back against the wall, too stoned to move, nothing on but his shorts, for hours on end.

Wrestling around with Brook was a risky thing to do, I knew—not least because I couldn't keep something besides my competitive ego from flexing when we did. (Jesus! What if he notices? But he never did.) And it left me feeling guilty, it was such a sneaky, depraved thing to do. I felt worse about it when I would see the older bachelor faculty residents of the college trying to pick the same kind of friendly fights. They never fooled me. I knew exactly what they had in mind, or I thought I did. And when I saw myself acting like that, a perverted dirty old man of thirty-one—the future looked bleak.

Although I knew what these resident perverts had in mind, and what the counselors in my boys' camp had in mind, and what the teachers in my high school had in mind, I would never have gone to them to talk about it. They would have vigorously, if not violently, denied it, just as I would have. These were the last people I wanted to confide in, let alone have a relationship with. I wanted to ride around Wyoming with Tommy or Brian or Chip or Hank— not sip sherry with some pudgy, hairy old faggot. I was terribly intolerant, but they were terribly threatening to me. They were everything I was afraid of becoming.

Among all my fellow Yalies, surely there were others like me. There had to be. To find one!

I even thought of sending "sexual preference question-naires," marked "highly confidential, entirely anonymous," to my 1,000 classmates, or perhaps to just a few. We frequently received questionnaires of one sort or another. I would send mine out on forged Psychology Department letterhead and have the business reply cards return to a post office box registered, naturally, under a phony name. The "anonymous" questionnaires would have been preprinted with a code that showed up under ultraviolet light. Brilliant, no? The scheme was sufficiently foolproof for me to consider it every so often, and sufficiently preposterous for me never to summon the nerve to try it out.

In our college we did have one "avowed homosexual," Jon Martin, a student in Brook's class and one of his good friends. Brook could afford to like this lisping, shrieking long-haired kid, because Brook was at peace with his masculinity. Jon was particularly threatening to me because along with exposing himself as a homosexual, he had taken it upon himself to expose everyone else. He talked constantly of "closet cases" and "closet queens." He believed in liberating the world. He thought it was sick and hypocritical to hide one's true sexual preferences—so anyone who got involved with Jon could not be assured of having his confidences kept.

I dumped on Jon Martin at every opportunity. I was an Uncle Tom, a peroxide-blond Jew with a nose job and blue-tinted contacts who persecuted other Jews to keep the Nazis off his back—a schmuck of the worst order—but I had to dump on Jon Martin all the same. What would people have thought if I had befriended him? If I had even laughed when he "camped it up"? If I had looked interested when he talked about the gay bars he had been to—or asked him for the address of one? Tommy would have been disgusted by Jon's antics, so I was disgusted by them. Hank had no use for an oddity like Jon, so I had no use for him.

In fact, I realize that my near hatred of Jon Martin was genuine. Here I was centering my being on the cosmic feelings I had and the burdens I bore, here I was carefully cultivating all traces of normality and masculinity—and here was Jon Martin spitting on the temple, laughing at closet queens, ridiculing my entire value system. He was saying that the Great Scorekeeper gave points for being yourself, for being honest—not for being a consummate, cosmic phony. He was saying that all my effort and pain of the last several years had been laughable. I could not accept that, so I was repulsed by Jon Martin, and dumped on him and his mixed up value system, his lisp, his swish, at every opportunity.

There was no way I was going to go to someone like Jon to tell my secrets and unravel all my knots. These were knots I had managed to live with for ten years and would manage to live with for the next forty. Whatever pain they gave me was unavoidable, and there was always the cosmic depression that they afforded.

But if only—if only I could somehow find someone like Hank or Tommy who had my same inclinations, my same fantasies. There had to be people like that. It was just a logical impossibility to find them. There was no way each of us could be sure about the other before talking honestly.

I felt a little like the character in one of those totalitarian stories—*1984* or *Animal Farm* or *The Grand Inquisitor* or *We*—the character they have somehow forgotten to brainwash, the one for whom ignorance is somehow *not* bliss. There must be at least a few others out there like you whom they have also missed, who have the same odd ideas. But spies and informers are everywhere, so in order to keep from having your brain amputated, you act and talk exactly as though you were like everyone else. But you desperately want to find your fellow oddballs. How do you find them? How do you communicate in a way only they will understand? If you tell the wrong man, you are zapped.

And who hasn't heard stories of plainclothesmen inviting eye contact with homosexuals, making friendly conversation with them, agreeing to go back to their places for drinks—and then busting them on morals charges that ruin their lives?

Even if stories like that weren't true, my self-respect would have been destroyed if I admitted the truth to a sympathetic, but straight, friend. And my perfect record, ten years of absolute loneliness and silence, would have been broken. And then what would the best little boy in the world have had? Neither normality nor martyrdom.

If only . . .

I graduated from Yale. With honors, naturally. I had been a moderate big shot on campus. The future was golden. Everyone told me I could write my own ticket. But where?

A few things were automatically ruled out. I would not do anything even vaguely related to art or hairdressing, because you know what kind of people do that. I would not try politics, because you need a pretty wife and adorable kids for that—or at least you have to like cocktail parties and $100-a-plate dinners and dances and socializing, always with a date, and I was not up to that. I couldn't expect Hank to keep me in blind dates forever. Of course, to a lesser extent, that would be a problem in any field. To get ahead, you have to socialize; to socialize, you have to have a date; to have a date, you have to know a girl who will go out with you; and to have a girl go out with you, more than once, anyway, you have to have sex with her. Or so I thought.

I was very sorry to leave Yale.

Hank was going to Paris to take a postgraduate year in political science prior to becoming a United States Senator. (That was my goal for him, not his; I was sure he could make it. I would be his campaign manager.) I couldn't think of anything to do in Paris.

I would have loved to move in and smoke Acapulco Gold with Brook, who still had two years to go at Yale, and with Fred, who still had nothing on but his shorts. But what kind of career could I build in New Haven? Career, after all, was a key word. I had no intention of falling behind, "handi-caps" notwithstanding. I had become too accustomed to sit-ting on wicker weave to settle for anything less.

I received a number of job offers, including one tentative one from the government known as a "preinduction physi-cal" notice. From the time the notice arrived until the morning of the physical a month later—that's six o'clock in the morning in case you didn't know—I could think of nothing else. For a combination of selfish and ethical rea-sons, I had decided that I would leave the country sooner than be drafted. Would my varicocele be enough to keep me out? Would I "check the box" on the long list of defects and depravities they handed you—the box next to "overt homo-sexual tendencies"? And then what?

I stumbled into the giant Whitehall Street draft center at five forty-five feeling much as I had in that Tossa hotel room. Everything was coming together this day. All my knots, tightened to the point of strangulation, were to be exposed to a bunch of unsympathetic crew-cut drill sergeants.

From six to seven we stripped to our shorts and stood in line waiting to be weighed. Standing in line with 1,000 naked black, white, and Puerto Rican strangers, all disgustingly normal-looking, who did not get embarrassed in situations like this, not a virgin in the crowd but me.

At seven they discovered that I weighed 151 pounds. By eight they knew I was five nine. (In elementary school I had been third tallest in the class—remember how important that was?—but my Naderlike pace in high school robbed me of sleep and stunted my growth.) By nine o'clock they had a vial of my blood and my chest X ray. Next they wanted a flask of my urine. I can't piss when anyone else is around.

I had always been able to piss like everyone else until shortly after that experience in the American Museum of Natural History. Some weeks later I was in the men's room of a New York movie theater. There were men pissing on either side of me, and I thought I saw one of them noticing me. That made me think of the man in the museum, and all of a sudden I could not relax. If you cannot relax, you cannot piss. It is as simple as that. I thought of my Big Secret, of my varicocele—this had never happened to me before!—and I got very embarrassed about the people waiting behind me to use the urinal. What was the Great Phonifier *doing* to me? I zipped up, having to piss more badly than ever, tried to look relieved, and left, feeling sorry for myself. From that day on, I could not piss whenever anyone else was around, or even if I thought someone might come in while I was trying.

Now, I wasn't stupid. I knew more or less what was happening, that I was psyching myself out. HEY, ADAM'S APPLE! CHOKE! I knew all I had to do to piss was to relax and not think about how embarrassing it would be if I couldn't. But I could no more keep myself from thinking about that than I could fall asleep by *trying* to fall asleep.

College football games had always been the worst. Sitting for three cold November hours on a cement stadium seat fills anyone's bladder. Though I had learned not to eat or drink much at the pregame cookouts—"What! You don't want a brew? Come on, have a brew!"—I still would have to take a leak at half time. Me and 10,000 other men of Harvard, or in this case Yale, all lined up along a hundred-yard partitionless urinal, all looking at me. The stadium had no stalls, just the urinal. What if my bladder actually burst one day? Surely that was a physical possibility. Balloons burst; bladders must burst. Or what if I doubled up in a cramp on the way back from the game, passing out from the pain, only to have the doctors diagnose it as a severe case of suppressed homosexuality? I learned to relieve myself at the crucial point in the game, when no one in his right mind would tear himself from his seat. Better to be thought soft on football than to explode in the stands.

By now I know that I was simply "Pee Shy," that millions of people are, and that it is nothing to worry about. That knowledge has gone a long way toward helping me relax, and I'm not nearly as Pee Shy as I used to be. But standing at the draft physical in front of a long trough with a paper cup in my hand, next to hundreds of naked kids with their things out, pissing merrily away, and others waiting to take my place at the trough, and all of them, no doubt, watching the freak show that was me tickling my penis to relax it, but knowing I didn't have a prayer—I just didn't have a prayer. I went to the nearest drill sergeant and said I couldn't piss in front of other people.

How was I to know, too embarrassed and guilty ever to have told anyone of my hangup, that they had instructed this guy: "Look, Joe, somathese little peckers won't be abladoit without goin' to the can. You stan' here and whennay ask you, tell 'em the can's over there. Got it?"

Before I had gotten my sentence half out, he pointed over there to the can. I went into one of the stalls, locked the door, filled the paper cup, and sneaked back into line.

By eleven they knew I could see well enough to shoot gooks and that I could hear well enough to duck when mortars were headed my way.

At noon we were allowed to get dressed again. They gave us a ticket we could exchange for food. I just walked around the block once and then sat down to wait.

At one we were given a mental examination. I passed. I had heard that it didn't do any good to flunk if you had gone to Yale; they wouldn't believe you. Then they gave us the list of Depravities and Gross Defects. Had I ever had a venereal disease? Hah! Was I an epileptic? A diabetic? Was I fatally allergic to Beegee buts? (I had a friend who got out on that.) Did I have any false limbs? Transplanted organs? Was I a hemophiliac? Had I ever been convicted of a felony? There must have been at least a hundred things on the list, all of which I checked "no," in the left-hand column. It made a long neat column, everything lined up just so. Except on number 93, I think it was—was I homosexual?—I had faintly checked "yes," which stood out of the column as though it were lit in neon. I erased it and checked "no." Then I thought of two years in the Army, where they have no doors on the latrine stalls and I wouldn't be able to piss for two years, and I checked "yes." But I thought I might be able to get out later in the day on my varicocele, and it would be the height of folly to check "yes" unnecessarily, so I erased it again and checked "no." I finished the last few items, then thought of everyone going on leave in Frankfurt or Saigon or Honolulu and running to the nearest cheap bar to buy a good lay, and them all wondering how come I wasn't horny enough to do that after two months of being around nothing but men—and I erased "no" and checked "yes." Ten-year perfect record, martyrdom, thrones, "no." My ethical aversion to the war: I would say it was better to have *pretended* to be homosexual than to have gone to jail or given up my citizenship, "yes."

I don't mean to bore you. Generally I finish true-false tests as fast as anyone else. This time I was the last to pass mine in. I had compromised. I had checked "yes," but crossed out over it and checked "no." I figured that if my varicocele didn't get out, I would appeal on new grounds. And when they saw that I had struggled over number 93, it might be easier to persuade them that I was for real.

But I could just see it, in front of three doddering, faggot-hating draft judges sitting in uniform at a small table with Old Glory off to one side, an Iwo Jima replica at one end of the table, and at the other end a screaming lavender telephone, their hot line to the Supreme Court of Brewster, New York. If I was a homosexual, it was their duty as red-blooded American fighting men to despise me. If I was not, I was a draft evader, and nearly as despicable.

No, that's not the way it would go. These men would be gruff but understanding, and my obvious embarrassment and good manners would disarm them:

"Well, son, you don't look like a homosexual."

"Thank you, sir. I am, though, sir."

"Well, then, we won't drag this out. Just give us the names of three or four gay bars in New York by way of a sort of proof."

"Ahhhh. I can't, sir."

"Really? But your file says you have lived here almost all your life. Surely if you were a homosexual, you would know these names?"

"Yes, sir, but I don't."

"Well, then, give us the name of your psychiatrist. You really should have brought a letter from him to your preinduction physical and saved us a lot of time. What's his name?"

"I—I, uh, I don't have a psychiatrist."

"Well, then, the psychiatrist you used to have or a doctor you may have told?"

"I have never told anyone, sir."

"Come now, young man, we are too busy to play games. You say you have been a homosexual since you were eleven and . . ."

Another impossible case for poor F. Lee Bailey. Is it possible that I would now be hiring him to prove that I *was* a homosexual, after all my elaborate ruses to conceal that fact?

The point is, I thought that if I ever had to try to convince the draft board that I was gay, the fact that I had checked number 93 and then crossed it out might somehow help. *I* didn't know what the hell to do, sitting there on Whitehall Street with that god-damned true-false test!

The afternoon wore on, and I was passing everything but water with flying colors. I asked to see the psychiatrist. They put me at the end of a long line. Before my turn came up, they told me it was time to go to the final desk for what I gathered was kind of the wrap-up, do-you-have-any-objections-or-forever-hold-your-peace desk. This is where I had been told that I would be allowed to display my enlarged scrotum. Nowhere else on the assembly line were they programmed to notice it. At four o'clock—a very long day—my turn came with young Dr. Heathcliffe on the wrap-up desk. He told me he had all my test results in the file, there, and I looked okay. Did I have any last words? I said I had a varicocele. He told me to go sit down in a room off to his right. He would be in in a minute to look at it. Privacy! Well, almost. There was another kid in there; evidently a troublemaker. He had refused to cooperate somewhere along the line.

Half an hour later Dr. Heathcliffe came in. How much longer could all this drag out? The other kid, a Puerto Rican, offered Dr. Heathcliffe some physician's letters, but a sergeant came in and said he had been a wise-ass. The kid said something to the sergeant and to Dr. Heathcliffe having to do with their collective mother. The doctor ignored the physician's letters, whatever they said, and stamped the kid's file OKAY. He was in.

Then Dr. Heathcliffe looked at me, the soul of a respectful, well-mannered white young man—not unlike Dr. Heathcliffe himself a few years back, one suspects—he looked at my varicocele and asked whether it hurt. I was working up the energy to lie and say it did:

"Well, uh—"

"Yes, I imagine it does. It's quite large. Okay." And I was out, never to hear from the Army again.

I had applied to Harvard Business School and was planning to spend the next two years there, not so much because I wanted to be a businessman as because law school sounded like too much work and medical school was out of the question. I knew a lot of my friends from Yale would be up around Boston, so there would be an ample supply of people to idolize. And a Harvard MBA was the kind of thing you would expect the BLBITW to have. What could be straighter than a Harvard MBA? Or more dull, maybe, but we all have to make compromises.

I was accepted by Harvard but then got an offer from IBM. I had gotten some help from them while I was working on my thesis—"Application of Computer Simulation Technology to the Determination of Optimal Airline Insurance Coverage"—and they had apparently taken an interest in a business type (my publishing exploits) who had some familiarity with computers (my major). They made me a tempting offer. An office with a view of Manhattan, half a secretary, and lots of money. It sounded like a shortcut in my rat race to remain the best little boy in the world, a jump ahead of my classmates who would be going on to graduate schools while I was climbing the corporate ladder. It also sounded reasonably safe. I couldn't picture IBM having weekend orgies out at the company place on Long Island, so I might not have to do much "social work" to get ahead. IBM's reputation for prudishness was attractive. I took the job.

I did very well. The BLBITW was indeed the youngest to

rise the fastest to the mostest ever, and all that. How did I do it? It was a simple combination of two strategies: the corporate politics and ploys of *How to Succeed in Business Without Really Trying*, plus really trying. I really tried, sublimating my sexual energy into my work, as usual. My boss would ask for a memorandum on such-and-such a topic as he was leaving to catch the 5:21 out of Grand Central on Wednesday afternoon. He expected to see the memo on his desk by Monday or, at latest, Tuesday of the following week. Hah! I would stay at the office most of the night writing the memo, typing it, Xeroxing it, binding it—and there it would be on his desk when he got in Thursday morning. That was as close as I could come to a sexual experience.

CHAPTER 6

I enjoyed my work, my blue-carpeted office, my IBM dictating machine, and my paycheck. But I was getting lonelier by the month. Almost every month, it seemed, especially that first summer after graduation, one of my college friends was getting married. It's not easy to fantasize riding the range with a married cowboy. Cowboys don't marry; they just pal around on the range and whore it up when they come into town. And the best little cowboys in the world don't even whore it up: Look at the Lone Ranger and his faithful Indian companion. Did you ever see them eyeing pussy on the street?

There was only one attractive guy my age at work, a healthy-looking Chicagoan come East named Rick Swidler. Gay, I learned years later. We would go out for lunch to the local Italian restaurant and talk about the sexual characteristics of the Italian women we had known. He did most of the talking.

IBM was a good place to work, but boy, did I miss Yale. I missed sweat shirts and jeans and track shoes walking past my library nook. I missed maneuvering for a seat next to that sandy-haired boy from Tucson I was determined to meet and "happening" to sit next to him in 100 SSS, striking up a conversation, meeting for a couple of beers at Mory's Thursday night, shaking hands when paths crossed at the Co-op. . . . And now I was getting an invitation to that sandy-haired boy's wedding.

Goliath, too, had long since gotten married, and it was getting to be my turn. My grandmother, subtlety personified, told me she would give me $1,000 when I got married, but I was holding out for more. My parents wanted to know when I would start bringing girlfriends up to Brewster for weekends the way Goliath had.

I would respond by changing the subject. My parents never pressed the point, but their anxiety over my finding happiness (and happiness is a family) was all too apparent, anyway.

I should have brought girls home, for my parents' sake. And I should certainly have dated in New York, to keep up appearances and to keep my hand in. I knew that the longer I went without a date, the more uncomfortable I would feel when I finally had to get one. The longer you put off your visit to the dentist, the more cavities he finds to drill. Yet without football games to require dates, and without Hank to supply them, I could no more take the initiative and inflict a date on myself than a little kid would take the initiative to visit the dentist.

How long could I go without dating—or *marrying*—before people decided I was queer? I had vague notions of two years in the Peace Corps: A series of letters home talking about this girl I had met in Nairobi; a picture or two sent; a sudden marriage which, for fear they would not approve of my marrying a Kenyan, we decided to hold in the jungle without family or friends (read: witnesses); a year of letters about how happy we were . . . and then tragedy. She would be bitten by a snake or smitten by leukemia—whatever seemed most plausible. I would be so grief-stricken I would not be able to remarry, or even date, for years. Maybe ever. The perfect alibi.

I shared an apartment at Sixty-third and York with an old friend of mine from camp, Jimmy Iskowitz, a college pole vaulter who looked as though he were put together from five sticks of Ronzoni spaghetti, with big meatball feet, hands, and head stuck at the ends. We had a view of Rockefeller University, the Cornell Animal Hospital, and the Fifty-ninth Street Bridge. It was a nice walk to work.

I have known Jimmy from the time we were ten, our first year at camp. Now he is one of the 4,000 assistant vice-presidents at First National City Bank; in camp he was considerably less dignified. He was one of the most active experimenters and one of the least embarrassed about experimenting. He never came right out and *said* he was experimenting; but everyone else said he was, and he would just grin.

Once when I was still at Yale, my last year, Jimmy was in from the University of Wisconsin, where he was an economics major, and he came up to visit me. We went to Mory's for a few drinks. After I brought him his third, I came right out and asked him: On a scale from one to ten, I wanted to know, where ten is totally straight and one is totally gay, just where did he fall? It wasn't a belligerent question. We were good friends, and he as much as invited it by joking around so much all the time. I felt secure asking the question because Jimmy knew perfectly well that I was ten on that scale. Hell, I wouldn't even let anybody at camp give me back rubs, for crying out loud. So I could sound a little curious without raising any suspicions.

After rambling through a lengthy preface, Jimmy said he was "about five" on the scale. (How could he *admit* that?) He told me that he used to mess around a lot at camp. Messing around meant sleeping in the same bed with somebody, beating each other off, maybe a few other things. Just the same stuff that has been going on at camps and all-male prep schools and British boarding schools for centuries, he said.

He told me that Tommy and Tommy's counselor used to mess around a lot and that Tommy would sometimes wake up to find his counselor in the same bed. He told me that the counselors who came back year after year, some of them in their forties and fifties, were gay. The camp bus driver was gay. Dan the Dishwasher was gay. Hell, my own counselor, Jack Simmons, for all his fancy dribbling and dating, would not exactly require all my fingers to count where he was on the scale, Jimmy said, though he wasn't sure just how many fingers I would have left over.

Jimmy himself hadn't messed around since camp, which was a long time ago. And he wasn't going to either. He wanted to become comfortably wealthy, belong to all the right clubs, throw the right kind of cocktail party at the right kind of Westchester estate, and be a trustee of the University of Wisconsin and the Museum of Modern Art. "Fiduciary" was written all over the gold watch chain that ran from the vest of his charcoal gray 36-extra-long suit to the suit pocket. And he was not going to let the urgings and stirrings of anything down around that pocket get in the way of a solid career in banking. It just took willpower.

Thus, for all intents and purposes, Jimmy Iskowitz was just as ten as anyone else, and I saw no reason not to room with him. On the contrary, I was glad to live with someone who wouldn't always be asking me why I wasn't out screwing. (I assumed he would not throw the first stone.) Someone, frankly, over whom I knew I had a certain power. His confessed desire for my athletic young body, despite his straight-arrow life plan, and my staunch refusal to let him come anywhere near it, somehow made me feel all the straighter. I guess I enjoyed the irony. It made my martyrdom more cosmic, if you see what I mean: his wanting to be ten but admitting he was five and wishing that I, ten, were five also, when I really was as one as I could possibly be.

Despite my involvement in my work and my good relationship with Jimmy, I was lonely in New York. I realized that most of my friends, maybe even Jimmy, would be getting married. And that pretty soon I would run out of college friends or camp friends to room with and would have to live alone. And that, while ostensibly everything was going great, the future was as bleak as ever, and getting closer fast.

I tried to take refuge in the past. When I took weekends off, it would be to go up to Yale and stay with Brook, my friend from Tulsa, and his roommate, Fred, who sat stoned in the lotus position.

This was my first year working in New York and Brook's junior year at Yale. Brook was in love with a freshman at Conn College named Debbie who liked to wear Yale T-shirts and jeans. She wore a size X-L T-shirt. In fact, if Debbie had wanted to, I'm sure she could have carried one of the dining-room trays on her chest without spilling a thing. Brook liked that.

Debbie would hitch down from New London every weekend to sleep with Brook. The dress and sex rules had fallen apart even faster than the economy the year after I left Yale.

Cohabitation was the order of the day. I had made it through just in time.

At least once each visit, I would ask Brook how all his friends were, including Jon Martin. The news about Jon usually included little stories about others and evoked conversations about homosexuality. I got the impression that Brook, a psych major, knew a good bit about the subject and that Jon was not the only one of Brook's friends in the college who liked other guys.

In terms of maintaining my cover, I should never have asked about Jon or engaged in these discussions. Sure, I always professed mild revulsion. But I have no doubt that this ruse began to wear thin when time after time I would lead the discussion around to Jon and homosexuality.

It was a risk I had decided to take. I would never *admit* to Brook that I was every bit as gay as Jon. But if he wanted to suspect, I would just have to let him. Because if we kept discussing this stuff, I just might find out who else besides Jon was gay. And that someone else just might be straight-looking, straight-acting, and straight-talking, like me. Hell, Brook knew so much about all this, *he* might be gay, Debbie's tray-table chest notwithstanding. He seemed to like wrestling around with me. I had read one of his psych papers where he talked about having been the shortest one in his elementary school class and how it had made him feel inferior. For all I knew, though Brook was now of normal height and apparent self-confidence, his sexual inclinations might have been molded in early childhood, as mine were. Of course, he was obviously not one on the scale of one to ten, or he wouldn't have been hunting for rubbers all the time. But that was fine with me. I was just hoping—it really was too much to hope for—that he might have been far enough down the scale to want to go off to Wyoming with me. Figuratively, of course: All I really know about Wyoming is that you can draw it with a ruler.

I was forever bringing Brook little gifts—birthday gifts, Christmas gifts, or gifts just because he was putting me up at his place, which made gifts allowable—and one day, my twenty-second birthday, he gave me one. It was the rock opera *Tommy*, performed by The Who. Brook said he knew how much I liked pinball, so he thought I would like *Tommy*. Tommy is "The Pinball Wizard, the Bally Table King." He is also deaf, dumb, and blind. He has no contact with the outside world, except a sense of touch. *"Deaf, dumb, and blind boy, he's in a quiet vibration land."* The doctors find that there is no physical explanation for his lack of sight, speech, and hearing. It's a mental block. *"There is no chance, no untried operation,"* says the doctor; *"all hope lies with him and none with me. Imagine, though, the shock from isolation, when he suddenly can hear and speak and see!"* Tommy's refrain is *"see me, feel me, touch me, heal me!"* He is desperately trying to break out of his shell. Midway through the opera Tommy is sitting in front of the mirror, gazing at his own reflection, but unable to see or hear his mother, who, becoming increasingly frustrated, smashes the mirror. Tommy is cured! His shell is broken! He is no longer alone!

I'm free! I'm free! And freedom tastes of reality.
I'm free! I'm free! And I'm waiting for you to follow me.

There is much more to it than that, of course. This is the part of the plot I choose to remember. See me, feel me, touch me, heal me. I have to think Brook had more in mind than pinball when he gave me *Tommy*.

In New York I was, as ever, thinking cosmic thoughts. One of the best times to do this was as I walked back home from work in the late evenings. I was certainly aware that there were hundreds of thousands of gay men in the city. Anyone knows that. But the men I could identify as being gay *looked* gay, and I wanted no part of them. I stared icily ahead and ignored every one of them.

Each time I passed Fifty-fourth Street and Third Avenue (and I made a point of passing that block every time I walked home), there were young boys standing in doorways or leaning against cars. I wasn't sure about them. What were they doing standing there like that? They didn't look gay, but they didn't look gainfully employed, either. Were they waiting to be picked up by women who would pay them? By men who would pay them? By each other? Or was this just the custom in the neighborhood to stand around like that? Were they waiting for the bus? I suspected that they were waiting to be picked up by men, but I never went up to any of them. What would I have said? Why would a guy in a suit carrying a briefcase walking up Third Avenue turn into a doorway and start talking to a rather unfortunate-looking Puerto Rican kid? " 'Scuse me, friend; got a match?" He either gave me a match or he didn't, and what then? "Thanks for the match. I haven't told anyone this before, but I'm a homosexual. What do I do?"

I must have passed that block a hundred times or more, but it got me no farther than Fifty-fifth Street.

And then another time on Third Avenue I was walking to a restaurant to meet my date and another couple. On the rare occasions when I had to date, I dated a lovely girl from my office who seemed to like me and apparently could live with my rule of never getting sexually involved with anyone from the office. (How was that for an excuse?) I was about three blocks away from the restaurant. I stopped at a corner to wait for the light to change, and I saw a remarkable thing that brought the adrenaline rushing. Two guys were standing at the corner, waiting also, talking to each other, unmistakably together. One was an absolute screaming faggot. He really was. He was wearing patent leather boots laced up to the knee, he had a pocketbook slung over his arm, his wrist was limp, he lisped, he stared at me—there was no question about it. He was almost a caricature.

But the *other* guy was so beautiful, young, handsome, I could have cried. He was wearing a blue ski parka and slacks, and looked as straight as Tommy or Hank. But he was talking with a homosexual, and when I got to the corner, he stopped talking and looked at me.

I looked back. Usually I would catch myself and not stare at guys. But he was *so* handsome, and he was looking deep into my eyes. I just stared, my jaw loosening and ready on an instant's notice to form any word I could think to say.

"Hello" would have been good enough. A smiled "How's it goin'?" could have changed my life. I really would not have had to be awfully creative. He had probably made loads of friends on street corners that way. It was nothing to get all choked up about. Just say hello, ask a question or two as you walk together across the street, discover that you are going the same place, and take it from there. Or even be honest: "Uh, I don't know how to say this—I've never said anything like this before, please don't take offense—but you wouldn't happen to be gay, would you?" Admittedly, nothing could be less sophisticated, more awkward. But even that approach, for all it lacks in manly self-confidence, has enough sincerity to pull you through.

And so what if it doesn't, for Christ's sake? So what if they both ignore you, or even run away from you, or just say, "No, buddy, we're not gay," or, "It's none of your fucking business!" So what? Is the Great Scorekeeper, the Great Policeman in the Sky, or the Supreme Court going to be any the wiser? And if they are, don't you think they already know your deepest thoughts? Get serious, for Christ's sake! *Relax*, for Christ's sake! Break out of the shell! Do it! *DO IT!*

The light changed and they started to walk across the street. I walked after them. Along with everything else running through my mind was the knowledge that three of my friends were waiting for me just a few blocks away. How could I go off to Wyoming when three people were expecting me for dinner? What would I tell them when I got back?

But mainly, I had no less than eleven years' worth of defenses keeping my mouth shut, flooding my brain with caution signals, and reminding me that my martyrdom, my wicker-weave throne—everything depended on keeping that inner shell intact.

They turned a corner. I kept walking, tears in my eyes, knowing that I had missed a once-in-a-lifetime chance to fulfill all my desperate yearnings.

Thinking back on it, I can hardly believe I could have missed the opportunity. I can hardly believe that anyone with half a brain in his head could get so totally wrapped up in his own martyr complexes. I mean, fun is fun, and if you can't find anyone, you may as well try to enjoy your loneliness—but here was my chance! Not a fantasy, a real chance! With everything to gain and nothing real to lose.

Jimmy Iskowitz got married. I could hardly believe that, either. But then if I, at the very tip of the scale, had been able to go for eleven years without having sex with a guy, surely he, closer to the center, could go forever with relative ease.

I really like the girl he married. Her sense of humor is as good as his, though he makes most of the jokes and she does most of the laughing. She is attractive in an unglamorous, unthreatening sort of way, sweet and cuddly, warm, with big brown eyes and Southern charm.

I was an usher in their wedding. After the wedding, I had no roommate.

That was in June, a year after my graduation from Yale, and well into my career at IBM. That summer, with Hank-for-Senator still in Europe and Tommy-with-the-tent-flaps-down married and Brian Salter and Chip Morgan who knew where, and Rick Swidler, seemingly straight, still friendly enough at the office but leading his own social life after hours—I made frequent trips to visit Brook, who was working in Washington. He and Debbie were semi on the rocks, and I think he was glad for the company.

One day in July—Washington swelters in the summer—we went out to a pool together. His sun-browned twenty-year-old's body, glistening wet . . . Most people, when they see something sexy, whistle or smile or get excited. I used to feel sad. It was too depressing to smile, too taboo to whistle, too impossible to get excited over, too sad to be cosmic. Oh, come *on* now: Was it really any worse for you than for anyone else, of whatever sex and inclinations, who sees someone beautiful and unattainable? Maybe not.

But if so, it was because I couldn't even show admiration, whistle, or say I loved him. Or even tell all my friends about him when I got home. It had to be pent up inside.

This cosmic martyr trip had been okay for the last eleven years. I doubt that those years were any less happy, on balance, than they are for most people; indeed, I am almost certain that the reverse is true, what with all my little achievements in camp, in high school, at Yale, playing and working all the time with cowboys of the first order.

But there is a time and a place for everything. We even recognize Red China when the right time comes, when we can swallow our pride, when we can shatter our mirror and break out of our shell. I was becoming acutely aware that the cosmic trip was not going to take me much farther. It was going to leave me all alone in a cave somewhere, with no cowboys, sitting in a lotus position looking down at my varicocele, feeling sorry for myself.

I visited Brook again in August. We met for drinks at one of those plush downstairs Washington bars. This time I told him. I told him because after eleven years of silence, I could stand loneliness no longer, I could stand pretending no longer, and I wanted to tell someone that I loved him. I told him because I felt the best years of my life were slipping away, working late at IBM.

With three drinks in me and more stammering and prefacing and blushing than I care to remember, I made the startling, astonishing revelation—that I liked boys instead of girls. I was shaking with adrenaline, and my teeth were chattering.

Thousands of times I had fantasized telling someone I was "a homosexual." (Which sounds so much worse than telling someone you are "gay.") And now I had done it, the record spoiled, birth given to the idea. But the rest of the fantasy never materialized. Brook did not stand up in surprise and disgust and shout, "A *homosexual?*," attracting the stares of everyone in the bar. Lightning did not strike. The floor did not even move.

He just listened sympathetically. Not sympathy for my homosexuality, but for the trouble I obviously had accepting it. His first question was: Had I seen *The Boys in the Band*?

No. I should, he said.

We talked for hours; rather, I talked for hours, telling the horrors of sleeping with Kathy in Tossa, Hilda in camp, the red crayon; Tommy, Brian, Hank. . . .

Brook said that he had slept with a few guys at college and that he wanted to be able to find some physical expression for the emotional "love" he felt for other guys. But that he had not had too much success. I guess he is "eight" or "nine" on the scale. What normal male *doesn't* have some locker room pat-on-the-butt feelings for his best buddies? Ten is an extreme, not a goal or a standard of desirable normality—no?

When the bar closed, we went back to Brook's apartment. I got undressed to go to sleep. He came over and put his hand on my shoulder. I felt awkward, embarrassed—he was thinking of me not as a friend when he did that, but as a homosexual, which made it different. I started to move away. I thought he was doing it not because he really wanted to, but because he felt sorry for me, and I was too proud for that. He wouldn't let me back off. He put his arms around me and hugged. I hugged back, confused but very hard.

He said he wanted me to get used to touching. He said that to a point, he liked contact with me—back rubs, lying on top of each other, wrestling around. He just didn't want it to go too far; he wasn't sexually turned on by me. That was the part, of course, that made me feel awkward—like one of the resident faculty members at Yale trying to pick fights with the attractive undergraduates.

So I can't say that I was at ease or that we had wild, glorious sex together. We wrestled around. But that didn't matter: I had someone to talk with. I was luxuriating in *honesty* for the first time in my life. And relaxing my defenses. Creakingly, haltingly at first, and not without second thoughts, yet letting my guard down all the same.

I could tell Brook I loved him. I did. He told me that though it was not sexual, he loved me back. Now I'll tell you something. He must have loved me in a way, or else he wouldn't have had the patience to help me through this rather critical period. It put quite a burden on him. He was, after all, the only person I had ever told. Whenever I had something heavy to say from then on, I would call—who else? I didn't have other friends to spread the weight around to, and there was a lot of weight in the months following August, while I tried to adjust to a whole new way of life, a whole new set of values, a shaking up of all my solidly entrenched defenses.

At first it was all I could do to say the word "homosexual" and its synonyms. It took months, literally, for me to get reasonably comfortable talking with Brook about what I thought and felt. I called and visited frequently.

Once around Christmas he was talking about the British girl he had met over the summer and about how he wished he could go to London for Christmas vacation to see her. He was embarrassed when I surprised him with a round-trip ticket. I told him I knew that in a way people didn't like to be given things, that it could ruin a relationship. But he would be doing me a favor if he would just accept the stupid ticket: I had so much damn love inside me that had always been looking for an outlet, and would he just grin and bear it and be the outlet? Brook understood. He accepted the ticket and thanked me once then and once when he returned. Neither of us has mentioned it since. Perfect.

Hank came back from Paris and was home in St. Louis. I found a business excuse to go out and visit. I had missed my ex-roommate a lot that year. Friday night we went to the dating bar to try to pick up a couple of chicks. Unsuccessful and sleepy, we returned to his apartment around two.

"Sit down, Hank. There's something I want to tell you." My teeth were beginning to chatter again; my palms were sweating like cold-water pipes.

"Say what?" he yawned, sitting down.

I looked down at my hands. "I don't know why, but I have always felt exactly the same way you have about sex, except you've felt it for girls, and I've felt it for boys. For as long as I can remember," I said, sneaking a glance at Hank, "I have been gay. I mean, I've never *done* anything. You're only the second person I've ever told. But I finally decided I would risk my friendships for a chance to open up. . . ."

So I opened up, and we talked until five in the morning. Of course, I assured Hank that while I loved him, I had long since repressed any sexual designs on him, and he was safe. He blushed.

Hank seemed moved. Unlike Brook, he had never had even the slightest contact with homosexuals except for brushing off the occasional approach. He had never thought much about it. All he knew was that there were some people in the world who were born boys but wanted to be girls and that they were kind of pathetic. But like Brook, the only reaction my revelation apparently evoked was the desire to make things easier. The first thing he did was to tell me he was amazed; next he told me it made no difference to him, that I was still his best friend; and then he asked whether I had seen *The Boys in the Band*. Or, for that matter, whether I oughtn't to see a psychiatrist.

I didn't think so. As a kid, going to a shrink would have caused me even more embarrassment and anxiety and would have robbed me of my cosmic martyrdom. I wouldn't have been the BLBITW, I would have been a disturbed child. And fourteen-year-olds don't just walk off the street into a shrink's office. Their parents bring them. My God! If I wasn't allowed to ride my bicycle out on the street, do you think I would have been allowed to be a homosexual? My parents would have been shocked and, mainly, awfully unhappy. They would have felt guilty, that they were "to blame"—which is simply ridiculous, because they have to rank among the world's best parents.

As for seeing a shrink now that I was old enough to go by myself and now that I had broken my inner shell—well, I still didn't think it was a good idea. After eleven years of thinking about myself for hours on end, day in and day out, I felt I had come to know myself reasonably well. True, I had steered clear of the clinical literature. True, I had been leaning hard on seemingly ridiculous cosmic fantasies, martyrdom, and the like. But I knew what I was leaning on. I knew the self-image I wanted. I knew what I was doing, in a way.

One thing I knew for sure was that I was not changeable.

Hypnosis, Freudian psychoanalysis, shock treatments, or just "the right girl" were not going to work in my case. Maybe for someone at "three" on the scale; not for me. From age eleven I had gotten hard when I saw pictures of boxers in *Sports Illustrated*; I had never gotten hard looking at *Playboy*. Quite the contrary: The best way I found to get rid of my hard-on when it might prove embarrassing was to fantasize sex with a girl.

Nor did I have any desire to "be changed." I had grown rather attached to myself over the years, screwball though I was. A me that liked girls rather than boys wouldn't be me at all.

If I *had* wanted to change, *then* I would have had a real problem, seeing as how it would almost certainly have been a lost cause, at $25 or $50 an hour, three times a week, for life.

"No, Hank, I don't want to see a shrink right now. I think I can work things out without one," I said, explaining about the unlikelihood of my ever "changing." "Do you think a psychiatrist could make you gay?" I asked.

"No."

"Well, I feel the same way, only in reverse. Sexually speaking, I'm probably just like you—only in reverse."

The dam was indeed broken, and I started pouring myself out with increasing frequency and ease to virtually all of my good friends. All were straight, as I expected; all were glad I had told them; and, some amusing awkwardness notwithstanding, all reacted well. Telling them made us closer friends. For my part, I was much more relaxed and happy, not having to think twice every time I opened my mouth. How refreshing to walk down the street with a straight friend and, while he was nudging and leering about the approaching girl, nudge and leer back about the approaching girl's date!

I have to admit, too, that I relished the initial expression of surprise that would invariably form on my friends' faces when I told them. It was confirmation that my masquerade had been convincing and that my masculinity remained, more or less, intact.

My straight friends seem pleased that I am honest with them. It shows that I really like them, as I really do—and who doesn't like to be liked? Telling them does make us closer. And it's not your average ho-hum conversation. I'm talking about something new to most of my straight friends. In many cases, I'm sure, they listen thinking mainly of themselves—their own playing around in camp, if they did; where they fall on that scale of mine; where they would like to fall; whether a shrink could change *their* sexuality; what it would be like making it with a guy; who else of their friends might be gay, if I was. . . .

But was I really? I mean, sure, I've been talking a lot about it, but the only foreign tongue that has ever entered my mouth has been Hilda Goldbaum's. Isn't it time for a little action?

CHAPTER 7

It was now February of that year of revelations, and I was beginning to run out of straight friends to astound. I had actually gotten to the point that I could speak the words with some fluency.

The economy had seen better days, but I was riding about as high in New York as a twenty-two-year-old junior executive could ride. My parents were awfully proud of me, which was what had always made me run in the first place. The only hints of concern they showed, in a very low-key not-to-be-pushy way, were: (a) that I was working so hard I was not having a "full life," which in a family like ours is the way intercourse is described; and (b) that I was maybe smoking a little too much grass, and mightn't it be bad for the genes I would pass down to their grandchildren? (Up to this point, Goliath and Goliath-in-law had not produced any grandchildren. It was beginning to look as though that might be my job.)

My parents' concerns were pretty well summed up one day about a year ago when I received in the mail a clipping from the *New York Times*. MARIJUANA IS LINKED TO DULLED SEX DRIVE, read the headline, with the text that followed too ridiculous to quote. My inimitable mother had written across the top: "LET IT BE A LESSON TO US ALL."

Yes, I was smoking grass. And I must tell you the most remarkable thing. After I had told Brook "who I really was" and all that, I started to get stoned when I smoked. It was the same $15-an-ounce shit, according to our source, and I was rasping it down my tender throat in the same awkward way. (Need I mention that the BLBITW had never smoked cigarettes?) But now I was getting stoned when I smoked it.

In any case, I was doing well in New York, and except for being a sex-starved druggie, was still the perfect son. But every time I talked with Brook, he would ask how I was *doing*—that is, what *progress* I had made. And I was wondering much the same thing. The new-found openness with my close friends was sensational, the handshakes were still great—but there is just no limit to human desire. Not to mine anyway.

I would read the bathroom bulletin boards. But I knew that even if I ever did chance to find a "Meet you here at 3 P.M. on the 23rd" sometime prior to 3 P.M. on the twenty-third, which somehow never was the case—I could not possibly show up. Was it possible that those floor-to-ceiling extensions the library had added to its bathroom stall walls were to prevent what I thought they were to prevent? Was it conceivable that those peep holes that had been bored in bathroom stalls all over the world had been bored for *peeking*?

The only practical course of action I could think of was for one of my straight friends to introduce me to one of his gay friends. But none of my straight friends *had* any other gay friends. Or at least none they knew of.

I went to see *The Boys in the Band*. Had it been shown in my high school or at Yale—*mandatory*, so no one would have to choose to see it voluntarily and thereby implicate himself—I think I would have had an easier time of things. And had I known then which of the actors in this movie were in real life straight and which gay, I would certainly have been given heart!

I am not saying I would have been encouraged to come out in any direct way. To be the powerful, hysterical movie it is—hysterically funny and just plain hysterical—an unrealistic amount of emotion and unhappiness must be crowded into a two-hour gay birthday party. But at least I would have learned a little about gay life, become familiar with some gay lingo. I would have seen a perfectly straight-looking, dignified pipe-smoking man who was gay, and that would have made an impression on me.

I went to see *The Boys in the Band* not so much to learn gay lingo as to meet someone standing on line or in the theater. I met no one. I think my problem was that I just couldn't force myself to look "inviting," however you do that. Well, I suppose a start at looking "inviting" would be to stop looking forbidding. What I looked like, I think, was a straight kid who didn't want any funny stuff from any of the queers who went to see this movie.

After *The Boys in the Band*, I secretly went to see a movie I simply could not resist. It was one of the first of the gay porno movies to be shown at regular prices in more-or-less regular theaters, off Forty-second Street. I couldn't resist it because the ad in the *New York Times*, no less, was for Andy Warhol's—That makes it art! An excuse if I'm seen!—*Lonesome Cowboy*. Need I say more?

I had a team of wild horses dragging me to that movie,

and another team of equal strength trying to drag me in the other direction. The reason the first team won was that I was pulling with them and tipped the balance.

Fortunately there was no line to be seen standing in, the ratty old theater was too dark for me to be identified; but it was just light enough for me to realize that the audience was almost entirely old men with overcoats in their laps.

Lonesome Cowboy was quite the turn-on. I snuck out before the end so as not to be seen, and left as Lonesome as ever, only, if possible, hornier.

Then one night in March, flying back to New York from a business trip, I read an article in *Esquire* that said something about the "Personals" in the classified ad section of the *East Village Other*.

On the way home, I bought a copy of the now-defunct paper, feeling guilty as I asked for it, as though the newsy could read my motive, and feeling stupid for feeling guilty. Sure enough, the personals were filled with groin tinglers, mostly for male "models" who would pose for nude photography, who were "butch," whatever that meant—I swear I didn't know at the time, though I got a sense of it from the word—who were "well hung," which I supposed to my embarrassment had something to do with that area down there, and who all had different names and measurements and hair colors in different ads, but who all had the same phone number. Hmmmm.

I called that number several times. Sometimes it just rang and rang. Usually it was busy. And sometimes a male voice answered. When that happened, I simply said—nothing. I was really going to ask some voice to come up to my apartment, right, past the doorman, maybe past the superintendent, maybe on the one night my parents would decide to drop in unexpectedly—and when this model got up to my apartment, I would take out my finger paints and my red crayon, right, and start to draw him in the nude. I was almost certain those models were never drawn or photographed, that they would come expecting to have sex. But there were an awful lot of people I didn't want to have sex with, so what if this happened to be one of them? Or what if he happened to be in the business of recording names and addresses and sending you little bills each month? Or of just coming over with a couple of friends and rolling you, for kicks? I would listen to the voice saying "Hello" and try to perform some kind of audio holography by picturing the whole person from just a voice fragment. It didn't work.

I finally decided to go down to the address listed in one of the personals—just show up and see what happened. I brought my wallet with plenty of cash and no ID.

It was a bright April day. I walked up the stairs of a warehouse-type building in the West Teens somewhere, into a room whose door was partially open. There was no sign on the door, but it was all so dingy and dark, with my pupils just beginning to adjust from the bright outdoors—I knew this was the place.

As I walked in, something in the stale air reminded me of a traveling fair that had passed through Lewiston, Maine, when I was a junior counselor at camp. Another counselor and I had gone to check it out, bet on the wheel and throw baseballs through tires, but when we got there, a barker was calling to us—it was a very small fair—"Come on, boys, show's about to start, last call to see Darlene do her world-famous tease, last call. . . ." I'm sure his patter was much raunchier than that; I had all but entirely repressed the whole experience, it was so awful. My companion, of course, was dying to see Darlene do her thing, and only a homo would have held back. The air inside the tent was nauseating. There were only a few other people inside gathered around a small elevated wooden stage. For twenty minutes more nothing happened as the barker kept exhorting others to hurry, hurry, hurry, the show was about to begin, and for twenty minutes I had to pretend that I couldn't wait.

Darlene came out, a tough, forty-year-old cocktail waitress type, and everyone crowded around the wooden stage. There was room for everyone to get right up close. Darlene stripped, which I managed to survive, until she came to the part that drew people to fairs like this one, the only part I really remember. She had everything off and had worked up a good sweat, and now she went to each of us in turn and grabbed our heads and stuck our noses . . .

That was the scene I flashed to as I walked in the door of this place—but I walked in. The room had a very high ceiling, black walls that were only flimsy partitions set up on the huge warehouse floor. There was a filthy carpet, worn bare, some ultraviolet lights, some unlit spotlights that looked like stage equipment, and one beat-up legless couch on the floor to my right. Two boys were sitting on the couch, one ugly and faggoty, talking on the phone, the other blond and normal-looking, looking up to see who had come in.

I asked for Randy, the name of the boy in the ad. The blond boy said Randy was out on a call and that he was Billy. Would he do? I stammered that I didn't know what I wanted to do, but that I had read the ad in the paper and that I just wanted to talk to someone and here is twenty dollars, I said, putting a crisp twenty on the arm of the couch. Their eyebrows lifted a bit.

The other boy was off the phone. I was sure it was he, and not Billy, who was wearing the perfume I smelled. It wasn't a sweet smell, but rather an unpleasant mildewy kind of smell. I was trying to avoid his eyes.

It must have been obvious to both of them that I was not a routine client. The faggoty one asked whether I wouldn't be more comfortable if Billy and I went into one of the private rooms. Private rooms? I sort of shrugged assent. Billy led me through a canvas-covered door that looked as though it had come from a stage set and into a cubbyhole off the main room. The cubbyhole was entirely bare. The same "carpet" covered the floor; but it looked even worse, and there were stains on it.

Billy sat with his back against the wall, and I followed. I assumed that ordinarily what happened in that cubbyhole was that the customer "had sex" with Billy, just how I wasn't sure, but I didn't feel like it. Billy, though about nineteen and blond, which were two steps in the direction of Cheyenne, Wyoming, was sending out the wrong kinds of vibrations. Billy's fingernails were bitten to the limit, and his fingers were strangely red and pulpy, almost as though he had just soaked them for two days in a bucket of water. He just didn't look healthy. Well, if nothing else, he looked as though he had been sitting inside a dimly ultravi-lit warehouse too long.

Still, I was not sure I didn't like him, and I was determined to make progress. He listened to my story and did not believe it. I suppose if at age nineteen this boy had already done everything there is to do, COD, no less, then it would be a little hard for him to imagine a twenty-three-year-old (I had just turned twenty-three, seconds are tick-ing, seconds are ticking) who had never slept with anybody, of either sex, ever. He had met, aged nineteen, guys who liked to get fucked with their heads in the freezer, guys who wanted him to piss on them, guys who wanted him to take them over his knee and spank them, guys who wanted to lie down and jerk off with the heel of his boot in their stomachs—but I am not sure he had ever had anyone come up to his "office" with a story like mine. Innocence was not his field.

But for twenty bucks he was willing to give me the benefit of the doubt. He said I should relax, it was easy to come out, and that I would do very well on Christopher Street. Is it possible that that was the first time I had ever thought about the expression "come out"? I suddenly had frighten-ing visions of some sort of coming-out party where everyone got dressed up in drag, God forbid. Or at least where I was the center of attention and everyone would be introduced to me, and I would have to make a little speech or tap dance or something. In any case, Billy didn't mind my not wanting to do whatever you do in a cubbyhole like that and offered instead to show me all the bars, like Danny's, on Christo-pher Street. I should come back that evening.

I said I would, said good-bye and thanks, and went home. I spent a busy Sunday afternoon trying frantically to decide whether I should really do it. I kept trying to figure out what it was about Billy that bothered me. I kept worry-ing that I might meet someone down there that I knew from the real world. There was really nothing to think about, of course; I was just scared.

I decided to call Billy and ask some more questions, like whether I would have to talk to people and what I would have to do—just to get some more assurance from Billy that I should really go through with it and "come out," which somehow seemed to preclude "turning back." You only do it once. This Sunday night with Billy the Kid?

Billy answered the phone, or at least I thought it was he. "Is this Billy?" No, he said, it was Randy, Billy would be back in a little while. I called back in a little while and Billy answered the phone, or at least I thought it was he, and he said, yeah, this was Billy. I said it was Neil calling about to-night. (That was the name I had used.) Who? Neil, remember? I was down there this afternoon? Oh, Neil! Yes, Randy had told him about me. *Randy?* But I was there with *Billy*, I said. No! *I'm* Billy, he explained. You were with Randy, with the blond hair.

I hung up. I was certain that I had been there with a blond boy who said Randy wasn't around but he was Billy and would he do—and now they were doing some kind of strange schizoid superwhammy on my fragile head. I changed my plans. This Sunday night I would watch *Bonanza.* Maybe next Sunday I would come out.

Several evenings thereafter, on my own, I went down to Christopher Street, which is not the easiest place in the world to find if you don't ask anybody—and you don't for a minute imagine that I would have asked anybody, do you? I walked up and down the length of that street, past Danny's every time, but I did not see many people. The ones I did see were like as not gay, but not the kind of guest you would want at your coming-out party—emaciated or emasculated or bizarre or forty-five trying for twenty.

I went too early. The New York bars don't get going, by and large, until eleven or twelve, and I was going around nine or ten. Too eager. Danny's was not crowded at that hour. I know, because it has huge glass picture windows where it should have had heavy gray don't-notice-me walls. I didn't go in. I just walked by like any tourist and glanced in each time.

"Oh, for Christ's sake," I hear you say. "You must be some kinda supershy wimp. Just go inna goddamn queer bar and see what happens. Worst thing, nothing happens. What's ta lose?"

I hear you say that because, looking back on it all, I hear myself saying that. It's becoming difficult for me to remember just how strong my feelings and fears were. One thing I do remember quite clearly: While I was shy, and paranoid on anything remotely connected to sex, I was no wimp. So watch it.

Why not just go in? Well, not counting the fact that there were huge picture windows, which had to be insane, there were more subtle reasons. Which of the two doors do you go in? Does it matter? If you go in the exit door, everyone will look at you and know that you don't know what you're doing. If you go in the right one, everyone will look at you, anyway: When was the last time a Yale sweat shirt and track shoes walked into a place like this? And that's another thing. I wasn't wearing a Yale sweat shirt and track shoes, but what *do* you wear to a gay bar? By and large, in New York, you wear jeans. I didn't happen to own a pair of jeans, cowboy that I was, because I could never find jeans that fit, which was always a source of mild embarrassment. I had run so much cross country in high school that my calf muscles were larger than standard tapered jeans. Remember tapered jeans? So I was wearing some businessman-type slacks, and everyone would have looked at me as if I didn't belong. Where would I put my hands if everyone looked at me? And where would I put my eyes? That was what it all boiled down to, I guess. I had a feeling that everyone would be looking at me from all sides, and where would *I* have looked? At the ceiling? Ridiculous. At the floor? Yes, but then why come in at all? Look back at them? God only knows what that could invite. And I had this thing about not looking back at queers, because I didn't want to be queer myself, I just wanted to pal around. You know.

I found and answered one of the *East Village Other* personals that sounded human. A student who was gay and looking to make new friends. An attractive student, the ad said, with a box number to write to. I wrote something about how I had never done anything like this before and asked him to give me a call. Unless he had connections, my phone number and first name alone would not enable him to trace me. I would have a chance when he called to think out my next move.

He did call, and suggested we meet at Googie's, a mixed bar he liked in the Village. Mixed? I asked. Yes, some straight, some gay—that's how the Village is. Oh. He sounded all right so I said okay. He would be carrying a black umbrella and wearing a black turtleneck, he said. What kind of person puts ads in the newspaper to make friends? I didn't tell him what I would be wearing, just in case I wanted to call it off when I saw him coming.

Up came the black turtleneck, right on time. (I was early, of course.) He was a little on the heavy side, nondescript, not terribly gay-looking or -talking, and nothing to be afraid of, so I met his eyes and nodded when he asked whether I was Neil, and we went in for a couple of beers. Would I like to come back to the black turtleneck's place for another drink? No.

As we had been talking, I had come to like him less. Of course, it was my fault, not his. He was polite, friendly, interested: a very nice homosexual theater student at NYU who wanted my tough young body. It just didn't work.

I tried to be as polite as I could and said no thank you. He was upset. Partly, I think, because he wanted me or, worse, the part of me we simply never discuss. Partly, I imagine, because I had just finished telling him that I had never in my life had sex with any human being—so my refusal was as much as telling his turtleneck ego that even a lifelong horniness would not be enough to make me jump into bed with the likes of him. He said something very homosexual-sounding—"Oh, don't I please you?"—which simply reaffirmed my resolve, and we walked in opposite directions: I back home to feel sorry for myself; he, no doubt, to Danny's to find someone else for the night.

I bought a new issue of the *East Village Other*—all of a sudden I was a regular reader, though I had never been to the East Village in my life—and I spotted a new cluster of model ads with a common phone number. I had been working late, as usual, in my carpeted little midtown office, and was now sitting in my swivel seat of respectability and professionalism, touch-toning the number of a male hustler. Of course I had checked to see that no one else was in the office.

Mike answered the phone as advertised. I had become somewhat bolder through my succession of unsuccesses—at least no physical or emotional harm had come from those earlier attempts—and way down deep I am really a practical business type anyway, so I just said, "Look. I know this will sound strange, but I am gay, except that I haven't been able to find anybody I like and I've never done anything. I don't really know what to do. I'm twenty-three, and I'm pretty good-looking and I would just like to meet you for a beer or something to talk."

Well, what do you know! I did it!

Mike was a little hesitant—hustlers have to be careful, or they may show up at the appointed place to find a small gang of faggot haters with short metal chains—but he agreed to meet me at ten o'clock outside Max's Kansas City.

He was already standing in a doorway next to Max's when I showed up in the charcoal pinstriped suit I was still wearing from work. I had told him I would probably be the only one around wearing a suit, for which I apologized, so it would be easy to recognize me, and it was.

Mike and I were both relieved when we met and shook hands. He was a regular guy: about 160 pounds with a strong handshake, a rugged, handsome face, wearing a thick-knit crewneck sweater and jeans and boots, mid-twenties. He didn't talk like a preppie, but he didn't talk like a faggot, either. He talked like a bright, likable, regular guy. We went inside for a pitcher of beer.

The first thing he told me was that his real name was Dick Warren, that he just used Mike in the ads. I took the opportunity to explain that I had done the same thing and told him my real name. And then I told him everything else.

He had been worried about coming to meet me, he said, because the story sounded kind of strange over the phone. I told him I was really glad he had taken the chance. I asked him, well, essentially, I asked him what such a nice guy was doing in a job like this.

He had gone for a year of college, he said, but didn't like it. He liked to be outdoors, to work with his hands. He had had some construction jobs and had worked up in Alaska for a while; but now he needed the money, and this line of work wasn't as bad as I might think, though he was looking to make a change. He could take care of himself, he told me, and he didn't mind having sex with older men. He just didn't think about it much while it was happening, and he wouldn't let them do things he didn't want to do. Some of the guys he met were really attractive and successful. Dick had made some pretty good connections this way.

I had gotten only a few hours' sleep the night before and had gone through my share of two pitchers of beer, but I had never been more awake and keyed up than I was that evening. Do you understand? I really liked Dick, and Dick liked me, and he was gay too! It had taken me a dozen years from conscious desire to expected fulfillment, but, more or less, I was there.

Hallelujah.

Dick asked whether I would like to go someplace, and since I had a friend staying with me for a couple of weeks, I said we could take a hotel room. I had my deck of credit cards, so we went to the Americana. Thirty bucks for the room? I would have paid five hundred. Which is not to say I was all smiles and eagerness at the check-in counter. It was that hotel in New Haven all over again, as far as paranoia was concerned. "No baggage, sir?" What was worse, I wonder: taking a hotel room alone to fool your roommates into thinking you poked little girls, or taking a hotel room to make it with a guy? I was sure the Americana desk clerk saw right through me (Dick was waiting in the lobby), but I got the key anyway. I realize now that the desk clerk would probably have given two bellhops to skip up to that room and jump into bed with us, but at the time I had not developed much skill in telling who liked what.

After some pausing and looking around the room and switching on the Zenith defense mechanism and looking to see whether there was a 25-cent vibrator machine under the bed and whether the door was securely bolted and everything else to delay actually *do*ing it for the first time in my life, I sat down on the bed next to Dick, facing some asinine late movie. Dick really was a handsome guy, and I really was rather drunk, and with a little help from him we were soon hugging and rolling around and wrestling around and just feeling each other's muscles and gradually getting our clothes off.

It was great. Really, there have been few times since when I have had such good sex. Partly, of course, because the first time is always best. Partly, Dick was hunkier than many of the men I've been to bed with since. Mainly, I didn't know what I was supposed to do, so I just did what came naturally: wrestling around the way I had in camp and in high school and with Brook. Only now it didn't just last a couple of minutes, and now I didn't have to feel paranoid, and now I knew I was with someone who liked it too, and now we had all our clothes off, and now we were doing some things I wouldn't have done with Brook.

But not many things, and that, too, was what was so good about it. We weren't kissing (cowboys don't kiss!); we weren't putting our cocks, God forbid, in each other's mouths, or anywhere else, though we were touching places I had never touched or been touched on before, and touching so lightly as to drive my ticklish, nervous, hypertense body wild and into a vain attempt to pin Dick to get him to stop, and then wrestling around some more.

Perhaps the innocence of it all appealed to Dick. Being the rugged outdoors type, perhaps he didn't go for kissing, either, though I am sure that this was the first time in ages, or ever, that he had had sex without *doing* anything, for crying out loud. Dick's experience as a hustler had led him to be very flexible. A good hustler, I suppose, does whatever he thinks his customer wants, within reason.

The important thing was that it was not until later in my "development" that I realized Dick and I hadn't been *doing* anything. We were doing everything I wanted to do. And not feeling that there were other things Dick wanted to do, I wasn't self-conscious about just wrestling around.

We messed around for hours, and I wasn't even aware of, or at least I was not thinking about, the fact that generally what happens is you reach an orgasm and then quit for a while. Neither of us reached an orgasm, as a matter of fact, and eventually we went to sleep, around five. I had to be at work at nine for a meeting I had called. I left Dick with my phone number, waking him long enough to say I had to go but would call him, and THANK YOU VERY MUCH! I would have been happy to pay him, but he said I was a friend, not a customer.

I got to my office, grungy as hell, exhausted, gravel under my eyelids, my varicocele aching just a little—I was feeling pretty good, all things considered. Hot damn! I walked from the elevator to my office too quickly for anyone to notice how awful I looked and then did my best with electric shaver and Wash'n Dri to come out looking like my normal presentable-but-overworked self.

At the end of the day I went home and called Brook in New Haven with a progress report. Then I called to talk with Dick and to make plans to get together the next night. Someone else answered and said that Mike was not around. "No, the Mike whose real name is Dick Warren is out, but I'll take a message for him if you like." I left my name and number and went to sleep. He must have been out on a job, because he didn't call.

It took me a couple of days to get him. I couldn't tell whether he was calling me back when I was out or whether he just wasn't calling back. I began to feel as though I were being betrayed or at least mistreated, and then I finally caught him in and asked him to go out for a cheeseburger with me after work. He was hesitant, and I, neither then nor now much for subtlety, asked him why—didn't he want to see me again? Weren't we friends? I mean, you're not going to leave me *now*, are you?

That last little feeling-sorry-for-myself thought I kept to myself as he reassured me. I just didn't understand, he said: He did like me; but he had to earn some bread, and he couldn't afford to spend another night with me, because he didn't want to take my money.

I fell over myself with understanding and relief, saying for Christ's sake I would be *glad* to help him out because I would still be getting by *far* the better end of things—and as the subject of money was awkward for both of us, let's just not *think* about it, and *please* meet me for a goddamn cheeseburger.

He did, wearing the same clothes as before. Maybe he couldn't afford much of a wardrobe, I thought. We had a relaxed, pleasant meal, cheeseburgers and beer. I gave him a check for $50 and said let's not even talk about it, just leave it at this: I liked him a lot, and he had done me a world of good, for which I was very grateful.

We went back to the Americana and played a rerun, only, as you would guess, slightly less "passionate," if you can use that word when nothing is *happening*, because it was less of an adventure. But I liked it, I thanked Dick and said I hoped I would see him again, and I left to go to work.

It might be a while before I saw him again, Dick told me, because he was going down to Haiti with someone; he wouldn't tell me exactly why, and he didn't know when he would be back.

I can't say I was crushed when I sensed I would likely not see Dick again. I did like him a lot; but the hustler thing bothered me, and I realized that if the second time wasn't quite as good as the first, the third time might not quite equal the second. I was beginning to feel a little more confident, also. To my amazement, Dick had said I was real good sex—but I didn't *do* anything!—and he said he didn't believe I'd never been to bed with anyone before. (Since then, I should quickly add, I have gotten only mixed reviews.) There was no stopping the kid now. Hell, I was good sex! Dick, himself as good-looking as they come, liked me and said I had a dynamite body (but maybe I should buy a pair of jeans). I was on my way.

CHAPTER 8

I decided I had had it with New York, I had had it with working fourteen-hour days, and I could not come out in the city in which my parents lived. I told IBM I wanted to take the summer off and then to be assigned to a job I knew was coming open in the Boston area. IBM raised a corporate eyebrow, but went along with it.

Guess who was living in Boston. Hank! Hank was entering Harvard Law School, which neatly fit my plan for him to become a Senator. He was living with his girlfriend in Cambridge. And Brook! Brook had finished Yale and was starting work in Roxbury as some kind of community organizer.

I took an apartment not far from Hank's and spent a lot of time helping to usher in the summer, walking all over Cambridge and Boston, looking up old friends from Yale, digging in.

Within two weeks, Hank had introduced me to a friend of his who ran a coffeehouse in Harvard Square, an old high school friend from St. Louis who I thought just might be gay. My in. Hank said, no, so far as he knew, his friend wasn't gay. Well, then, what about Hank's friend's friend, whom we had met in the coffeehouse, one Oscar Lipschitz?

Oscar was gay, no? Hank didn't know but promised to try to find out.

And here's to Mr. and Mrs. Lipschitz, wherever they are, for naming their only son Oscar. What's short for Oscar, who, now that I think of it, was quite short himself? Had they not done it, Oscar might have been out poking little girls at the very time I needed him to show me the scene.

The last thing I mean to do is to make fun of Oscar, a terribly nice guy who teaches underprivileged kids English. His students love him. I highlight his name and height because I presume these two factors had something to do with his turning out gay. ("Life ain't easy for a boy named Sue," goes the song.) And I am naturally intrigued by the general subject of what makes people gay. Of course, no one knows for sure and different people are gay for different reasons—but some patterns do seem to emerge.

Not that any short person named Oscar Lipschitz would grow up gay. Like "the boy named Sue" in the song, he could have grown up tough and ornery and mean—except that there must have been other circumstances, such as, perhaps, his height, that caused him to develop differently. Perhaps because he was small, he couldn't fight back when kids teased him, and he began to feel inferior and to idolize the same kids I idolized, if for different reasons.

There is nothing predictive in this, except perhaps to the extent that there may be a greater *probability*, if still a fairly small one, that short people with funny names, or tall people without fathers, or medium people who were overly sheltered, will turn out gay.

Anyway, Hank ascertained from his friend at the coffeehouse that Oscar was indeed gay. The next time I ran into Oscar I let it be known that, well, that I thought I probably wanted to meet some, uh, gay people, and, well . . . Oscar took it from there. He put me more or less at ease as we walked back to my apartment and he there spent several hours telling me all about Boston's gay scene and about his own way of handling it. He said he would be glad to show me around to all the places and to introduce me to some other people.

He also blew me—or tried to. He worked at it for an incredibly long time, reassuring me, entreating me to relax, telling me how good it would feel. But the more he sucked, the more upset I became, partly at the picture of the situation in general, and that I could be party to such a thing; more specifically, because I couldn't come. I realized then that I hadn't come with Dick, either. I was vaguely aware that *everyone* came when he had sex. Not only was I abnormal in liking guys—maybe I was even abnormal at doing that! I was supposed to like this, but I didn't. And, as usual, I was still too uptight to come out and say what I was feeling—to be completely honest and admit my fears. If I had, Oscar might have told me all kinds of stories about how it's hard for *everyone* at first (a harmless exaggeration), about how it might take me three or four weeks or even months of practice before I could relax enough to enjoy it and come, and that some of his best friends didn't like blow jobs anyway.

Oscar finally faced reality and bicycled home. I ran for the shower. If everyone showered the way I did that day, the Dial Soap people would rule the world. In my family we didn't believe in God, so cleanliness had top billing.

Oscar took me to Sporters, only a few hundred yards from the Statehouse, at the foot of Beacon Hill. He told me I should take off my glasses. Except for occasional wire frames, which look good on the right people, you don't see glasses in gay bars. I would have taken them off anyway—I only wear them when I drive—but that helpful instruction made me self-conscious. I get it: The idea is to saunter in there cool and attractive and masculine, like a gunslinger coming into a saloon in a strange town. I walked into Sporters as confidently as a man walking up to a podium to address a hostile audience on a subject he knows nothing about.

Having never before walked through a door like that, I would now walk through them on and off for the rest of my life.

Despite myself, I was a hit. I was a "new face," a young face, a face that was attached to a sweater instead of a body shirt—possibly *not* because it was attached to a lousy body, but possibly because—joy of joys—I was still fresh and innocent in the ways of gay dress and genuinely collegiate, not make-believe collegiate.

It was a Friday night. We had purposely come early, around ten, so the bar would not be too crowded. Later it would get so you had to push and press your way through bottlenecks of people, brushing away occasional stray hands, to find a few feet of space to yourself.

Why did everything get started so late, I wanted to know. What of the people in the bar on a Tuesday night who had to get up at seven the next morning? Oscar told me that the bar wasn't nearly as crowded on weekdays. Some of the weekday crowd were unemployed, were students, or worked odd hours, like waiters. Others had fallen into the routine of napping for a few hours after work, going to the bar, and then napping for a few hours before work. Those were the people who seemed to have lost control of their lives, he said. Sporters was open from noon to two in the morning, 365¼ days a year (except Saturday nights until one—blue laws), but Oscar suggested that I not bother with it before ten thirty or eleven any night but Sunday. Sunday it gets crowded early. (Everyone knows it does, so they come, so it does.) A lot of people come in Sunday afternoon because a brunch is served free.

Oscar offered three explanations for the lateness of gay life (late the world over). First, he said, by cavorting when all "decent" people were at home asleep, gay people were not likely to be discovered by their decent friends. They had the city largely to themselves. Second, the late hours permitted you to take your girlfriend to dinner and a movie, if you were into throwing your friends off the scent, and then run down to the bar for what you really wanted. Both these explanations would have pertained more to gay life some years ago, when people were even more uptight about being "discovered" and when society was even less tolerant. But having developed this way, there was no reason for custom to change—particularly because of Oscar's third explanation: It doesn't do to be one of the first ones at the bar. You look too eager. And if you are looking for a lot of people, why bother to go until it gets crowded, which everyone knows is late?

And there is still a fourth reason: Many people go to gay bars with the idea somewhere in their minds of taking someone home for the night. And many of those agreements are made as the bar is closing, at two. Sure, if two people really hit it off, they can hit it off at any time, anywhere. But more often, it's not so clear-cut. Neither party is anxious to be shot down by the other, and each thinks that maybe, just maybe, someone even *more* attractive is going to come over later on and slay some dragons for him—so, as in labor negotiations, it's harder to make a deal while there is still some time left. And it's harder to come up with good lines. A good line is handed to you on a silver platter at two when they close the bar. You *have* to leave; it's just a question of whether you leave alone or with someone. "Wanna come back to my place for a cup of coffee?"

Sporters had a drab exterior, no windows, and a tiny sign. That much I liked. Inside, it was dimly lit, with walls of mirrors and brick, and a red Formica counter running around the periphery. The place was basically rectangular, with the bar itself in the middle, and three bartenders in the middle of that. Once inside, you could walk all the way around the bar and come back to where you started. There was another rectangle, an open space, off to one side of the first rectangle, with a men's room and a ladies' room off that. (Use either, which I needn't tell you is a funny feeling.)

The first thing Oscar did as we entered was to buy me a beer (Carling Black Label, drink from the bottle) to give me something to do with my hands, something to look at, something to relax me. Like a barracuda attacking one of Goldfinger's victims, I scraped the label off in seconds. Had I been given a napkin with the bottle, it too would have been in little shreds and knots and crumbly balls. The beer was soon gone, and Oscar thrust me another. We were now halfway around the bar, Occupancy Not More Than 366 Persons—but the police who come in two nights a week for a beer and whatever, and who never ticket cars parked out in front in the bus stop, can overlook a little overcrowding. The last thing they want to do is to have to count a crowd of queers.

That early there were no more than 100 people in the bar, and every one of them, except for Mary, the octogenarian coat check lady ("fag hag"), stared at me as I walked by. Most of them were older than me (twenty-five to forty), and none was a cowboy. Well, there was one older guy dressed up like a cowboy, cowboy hat, buckles and all, but you know that is not what I had in mind.

I was sitting on one of the red-topped soda fountain stools in the other rectangular room, facing what I came to think of as the hippie area. This area ran from the jukebox on the right past the entrance to the men's and ladies' rooms in the middle of that wall, to the auxiliary bar on the left. It was as far from the entrance to the bar as you could get. Young men with shoulder-length hair, often bearded, a little spaced out like as not, stood in this area, not drinking much because 65 cents for a beer is a ripoff, man, when you can buy a six-pack for 99 cents or a tab of sunshine for $2.

As you moved away from that wall and into the center of this auxiliary rectangle, toward me, you tended to have a layer of people who liked hip types, but who were only a little hip themselves. Their hair was not as long; they were drinking. Or else they were people trying to make their way to the jukebox, which never ran out, ever, or to the men's and ladies' rooms. (Talk about Scylla and Charybdis! The men's room had no private places; the ladies' room had lockable stalls. I was too Pee Shy to use the men's room; too uptight to use the ladies' room.)

In the other rectangle, with the main bar, the average age of the crowd rose gradually on either side as you moved toward the door. Around St. Patrick's Day you even had some men in their forties and fifties getting smashed and dancing Irish jigs—but always on the left side as you entered near the door. You never saw these men in the back where I was sitting. Little neighborhoods were established by custom and maintained by a subtle pattern of smiles, frowns, glances, icy stares.

The lighting in the bar was uneven. Generally, the best-looking people chose to sit in the best-lit areas, though all the hippies, regardless of looks, preferred the darker corners in the back.

Nearly half the bar-goers were sitters who stayed put the whole night, either talking with friends or just watching as people walked by. A few sat facing the bar, backs to the crowds, drinking cosmic drinks with themselves. The other half, perhaps more, were cruisers, walking around most of the time and occasionally sitting down for a minute when a stool happened to come free, saying a few words to friends they passed, sending a glance or two at someone they would like to meet, engaged in the continuous effort to find that elusive White Knight—or at least some elbowroom.

The wall against which I was sitting was a good vantage point. It bordered a major traffic flow, and sooner or later everyone in the bar had to pass by. A lot of people looked as they passed, but very few came up to talk. Most didn't try to make conversation because when someone looked, I looked the other way. If two people were looking from different sides, I would look down at my beer. A few asked me whether I was from around here—oh, Cambridge? *I* used to live in Cambridge! But I was so icily indifferent to the fact that they used to live in Cambridge that none pursued it very far.

I wasn't playing hard to get; I was just nervous, shy, and turned off by all these unattractive people wanting me. I was getting ready to give up hope, around midnight, when I spotted a guy who looked just the way I thought a guy should look. Now the only trick would be to get his attention in that crowd of hundreds and somehow let him know that I wanted to be his friend and somehow convince him that, among all these people, and the friends he no doubt already had, I was worth becoming friends with.

What I did not think of at the time, and what took me a while to adjust to, was that by gay standards I was something of a hot shit. No one in the bar had been to bed with me, or even *seen* me before, and new young faces are at a premium at Sporters. No one was comparing me with the guys my own age, but with the whole group, of whom I'd guess I was in the youngest quintile. And then, too, I think it is a fair, though unfortunate, generalization that a smaller proportion of gay people than straight people are attractive. I had proportionately less competition. This is not to deny that many of the world's best-looking movie stars and athletes—and perhaps a majority of the world's best-looking models—are gay. It is rather to acknowledge two facts:

First, abnormal-looking people are less likely to have normal childhoods, less likely to have the self-confidence to make it with girls, and more likely to idolize the Tommys of the world, as I did. You have to think that the very short, very tall, very frail, very unfortunate-looking people you see in gay bars are gay in part as a consequence of their looks.

Second, gay people, however attractive their physical features and for whatever reason they are gay, live in a society which by and large shits all over gay people and tends to isolate them. Isolated, they have developed a subculture whose fashions and mannerisms and codes of behavior are different from straight ones. Shat upon, they may desperately wish they were different, they may lose their self-respect and with it their "manly" self-confidence. As a result, many fail to fulfill their potential by failing to pursue any sort of career. And many play roles they think they are supposed to play, lisps and all. Meanwhile, some overcompensate for being gay by dressing and acting supermasculine, to the point of attracting just as much attention and scorn as if they were in drag.

While there is little that can be done to make short people taller or gay people straight, there is much that could be done to change society's view of homosexuality. Understanding and acceptance would relieve much of the pressure that makes so many homosexuals miserable—pressure that causes the stereotypical behavior that causes the intolerance to begin with.

I think the reasons society is intolerant of homosexuality are not hard to imagine. Homosexuality threatens two things: propagation of the species and "masculinity."

Until recently, man always found it in his interest to multiply. The more sons a man had, the more likely they would have the strength to support him when he could no longer do so. The more sons in a tribe (and the more daughters, the more grandsons), the better chance the tribe had to defend itself or to conquer other tribes. Just a few years ago China was rewarding people for producing babies, a national goal. The process of evolution, by definition, favors heterosexuality and would, if anything, tend to discourage homosexuality. The simple fact that we now have too many people on the earth—that, in fact, the population explosion is suddenly at the root of most of the world's problems—does not abruptly change the attitudes and instincts we have developed over tens of thousands of years.

As for "masculinity," evolution favored those individuals

who stayed with the tribe. Evolution favored the tribes whose members cooperated. In order to cooperate, you have to have some guidelines, a little law and order, and the order was provided by dominance. The pecking order. Until recently, the animal that was dominant was the strongest, toughest, most threatening animal around. The more threatening you were, the more likely you were to get the prime cuts of beef, the more females you could have. Now it wasn't just how strong and tall and quick you were in a fight; it was how *threatening* you were, which is to say, how tough you *pretended to be*. (If it actually had had to come to a physical test each time, the tribe would have killed itself off in no time.) One ideal way to pretend to be tough was to dump on Jon Martin. Another was to deny your wife the right to a career or an equal say in the relationship. Another was to bully or at least disparage small, frail, "sensitive," or, generally speaking, feminine types. (What kind of credible *threat* to mobsters and Commies would the FBI be if the late J. Edgar Hoover and his lifelong friend Clyde had allowed women or avowed homosexuals to work for them?) You wanted the best for your sons, so you made sure they felt the same way, and dumped on Jon Martin, too.

I don't mean to suggest that all homosexuals are physically weak or feminine. That isn't true. The homosexual corporation president or drill sergeant is only shat upon if he *"admits"* he is a homosexual. (So he doesn't, so the stereotype is not changed.)

The women's liberation and gay liberation movements are saying—Look! Things have changed: A woman's primary function need no longer be to have the most possible babies. Look! Order should no longer be provided to the tribe by a baboonlike dominance hierarchy based on toughness, the threat of violence.

Anyway, there I sat at Sporters, not realizing the plusses I had going for me, and staring holes through the fellow I wanted to meet. That was, more or less, what Oscar had told me to do, only I realize now that he meant for me to be considerably more subtle. I just kept staring, feeling terribly pent-up and awkward, helpless, average-looking. It worked.

Rob said hi and I said I had been out (of the closet) for two hours. He asked me if I wanted to go home with him, and we pushed our way through the crowd to the door. On the way to his apartment in Back Bay he explained that he was, of all things, a computer operator on the graveyard shift of an all-night insurance-company computer installation. He was twenty, he had been out for about five years if you count his first parochial school experience, and he was planning to take a course in programming, which would pay a lot better and allow him to work daylight hours.

He shared his Back Bay apartment with a waiter, whose only distinction was a wig he had bought that day—a woman's wig—which made me exceedingly uncomfortable. How could Rob live with a moron like that?

I was already having visions of his moving out of such an unhealthy situation and into my Cambridge apartment, which was more than adequate for two people. I had known Rob all of an hour when I first suggested the possibility. I lacked perspective. Rob was the only one out of hundreds in the bar that night that I had liked. Surely I would have to take him away from there fast before someone else came over and horned in. If Rob was foolish enough to be attracted to someone like me, well, I wasn't going to steer him away.

I would say Rob, twenty, was three to five years older than I was at twenty-three. He knew where my head was; his had been there years before. He knew it would be safe to say, "Sure, maybe I'll move in—let's see what happens," because he knew I would change my mind within days, if not within hours.

As it happened, it was hours. The sex we had was not all I'd hoped it would be. It was upsetting. He wanted to do all the things gay kids do. He wanted to kiss (germs!); he wanted to put our respective things in our respective mouths (I had always counted: sixty-seven, sixty-eight, seventy, seventy-one . . .); and he even tried to, well, rob me of my virginity. That last was not only disgusting to think about, but was also, judging from what little progress he was able to make before I resisted, likely to be excruciating.

God damn it! Why can't I be like everyone else and like to do those things? What are people going to think of me? Is *this* what the Lone Ranger and Tonto did during the Quaker Oats commercials?

Rob didn't come right out and say that he was pissed off at me for being so stiff in bed; but I knew he was thinking it, and I felt sorry for myself. He said that I would get used to all those things real fast and that I would soon love them.

Now, I am by no means going to describe every tiny step I took on the way to lowering my inhibitions and having normal, uninhibited sex. I will say, however, that if the road to good sex extends from Lisbon to Leningrad, I am at the time of this writing lost somewhere in the Pyrenees, but hopeful.

There was a second reason I didn't ask Rob to move in

with me in Cambridge. In addition to his making me feel sexually inadequate, his verbal aptitudes were not equal to his math aptitudes.

I mean that quite literally. Remember, I went to a highly competitive high school and was supercompetitive myself, in the days when there were no pass-fail courses and when the stigma of asking a fellow student "Whaddya get?" was second in pain only to not knowing—so we asked. That is a must for anyone who is trained to be the best little boy in the world, for here is an objective, accurate measure of a boy's worth. Surely you wouldn't question the relationship between grades and personal worth? And in case you *are* one of those strange rebellious people who tended to pooh-pooh the importance of grades and to call them arbitrary and meaningless—that is, in case you are one of those miserable people who refused to play the game by my rules—well, I have an answer for you. The Educational Testing Service in Princeton, New Jersey. Its tests are scientifically designed and scored by *computers*! ETS is the Great Score-keeper in the Sky's agent on earth.

Therefore, as I was a lousy judge of people—people were never my long suit—I relied on their test scores to tell me just how smart or how dumb they were. I had this thing about what do you *do*, how smart are you—"are you acceptable?" I am not proud of the fact that I steered Rob's conversation around to the Scholastic Aptitude Tests, which are scored from 200 to 800 and anyone under 650 is at Yale because he plays good football, and I had never known anyone (but Brian, with whom I went to *Moby Dick*) under 500. Without having any idea of the importance I placed on it, Rob told me he had scored 705 on his math SAT, and 321 on his verbal.

This remarkable disparity, which I had never before encountered in anywhere near the same degree, was clearly borne out at our after-sex pizza. You could sense that Rob was intelligent (well, you knew he got 705 on his math boards, right?)—but he didn't say anything. What would be the point of living with an attractive twenty-year-old kid with whom you could neither sleep nor talk? Not even sleep with in the literal sense. Put me in a double bed with a shared sheet and the possibility of *touching*, and the inevitability that my half of the sheet will move when the other half moves—and you have one grumpy, groggy boy in the morning who has been up all night trying to fall asleep. Given all that, need I even mention that in a *single* bed, entwined in someone's arms and legs, I am no more likely to fall asleep than General Custer was when he saw the first million Indians coming?

CHAPTER 9

Rob did not move in, but he introduced me to Peter. Peter had a big smile, was a little on the cherubic side, twenty years old, and a tour guide. He was so much more gentle and understanding in bed, plus the strange things he did with ice cubes, that I made it with him several times before I lost interest. I even went on his tour of City Hall. Peter introduced me to Eric, who was going around the bar inviting people he knew to a party in Cambridge. "Cambridge! *I* live in Cambridge!" I said. Eric professed astonishment and delight at the coincidence—of all places for someone in the Boston area to live, Cambridge!—which just goes to show that it is the actor and not the line that makes the show, and I was invited.

There were probably a few nights in between Peter and Eric that I don't remember. Well, I was on vacation, and after my initial hesitation, I was coming out with a vengeance. It is enough to say that I was ready to have sex with anybody who turned me on, and as I was a new face, they were ready in return.

Why so promiscuous? Well, of course, there is the making-up-for-lost-time aspect. If I had taken five years to learn five years' worth of life, I would have been twenty-eight by the time I was, emotionally, twenty-three. And besides, why *not*?

All the taboos against sex that straight kids used to have, and some still have, no doubt have a lot to do with not making babies by mistake. The Pill was supposed to have revolutionized morals; well, I had something far more effective than the Pill.

Did the taboo against promiscuity have something to do with the danger of catching VD? But now VD is more easily cured than the flu, so "Even Nice People Get VD," as the ads say.

Also, what difference whether you have the stigma of being a homosexual or the stigma of being a promiscuous homosexual? If you're going to be stigmatized, the least you can do is enjoy it.

What I could never figure out in college, hornier than a rhinocerous, was why my friends didn't have sex every night. And in between classes. Why didn't a straight guy, when he saw a chick he dug on the street, simply say, "Wanna do it?" And why wouldn't she, if she dug him, say, "You betcha sweet ass"? Naturally, I was more than a little grateful for this prudishness, which protected me from impossible tests of my normality, but I just couldn't understand it.

In college I didn't know sex wasn't always the blissful, wildly pleasurable experience it was cracked up to be. That with the wrong person it could even get boring or distasteful. That there were other things in life. I *had* the other things, so I knew their limitations. It was only toward the end of that first summer in Boston that I began to understand and that my desire to be done by someone every night diminished (somewhat). It was only then that I began to form some strong relationships, to become emotionally involved.

I didn't become awfully emotionally involved with Eric, but a little. He lived right up the street from me. It turned out that he had gotten an economics degree from Boston College a couple of years earlier, so we had some common areas of interest. One reason I liked Eric was that he didn't go to the bar much. Instead, he was an organizer of Boston's Student Homophile League, which met at Boston University once a week, and he would organize gay touch football games on the Esplanade by the Hatch Shell, where he managed to reassure the hesitant ballplayers, like me, that we were all equally inept. Of course, we were not all equally inept, but everyone felt comfortable.

I got so I could talk intimately with Eric. I told him kissing made me feel awkward—"Cowboys don't kiss," I told him—and I told him how in my family, we didn't even put Goliath's spoon in my mouth—so how could I allow a strange tongue? Or worse? I told him about Hilda Goldbaum's French kisses with their Italian dressing. Just telling him these things helped relax me. He didn't get impatient or make me feel I was weird; he just thought I was funny—ha-ha likable funny, that is. Because I could relax with Eric, because I liked him and wanted to show it, and because the inside of his mouth always tasted like peppermint candy, I managed to lose some of my distaste for kissing.

As Eric was the first gay person I had ever spent much time talking with, he was the first one who made me formulate verbal expressions for what I had always felt. One common thing gay people do is to give each other girl's names—Eric would be Erica—and to call them "she" and "her" instead of "he" and "him." Among other things, this subculture habit helps avoid being found out: If your gay conversations are overheard, it is better to be saying you love "her" than "him." Whenever Eric referred to someone that way, I would punch him in the arm and tell him to talk right. So he only did it when he wanted to get a rise out of me. He knew I didn't like those of his friends who were noticeably feminine. He knew I didn't like it when any of his friends, including some of the most masculine, "camped it up," falsetto, where the *s*'s sounded like a radio that wasn't tuned in quite right: "Oh, my *dear*, how nicce your shirt looksss! I found one jusst like it in my grandmother'ss attic!"

When people did that around me, I turned icy. But why? One day Eric wanted to get a real rise out of me—I think I was falling asleep too soon—and he called me Trixie. He got a rise, all right. I told him, *Look, schmuck: if femininity were what turned me on, I would be straight. I like masculinity, so cut it out.*

Well, that was one way to put it, I suppose—and I have since put it that way on several occasions. But what I think I was really saying was: "Look, God damn it, I don't think I'm feminine myself, even though I like guys. Yet that's the stereotype—that deep down all faggots really want to be girls. Well, there is no way I ever want to look or act feminine. When you call me Trixie, you are threatening, even insulting. I have to demonstrate my masculinity by objecting. I am not willing to relax or to admit I am not just the tiniest bit superior, anyway, to all you queers who give in to looking and talking and acting a little queer, even if it's only in private among yourselves." My public relations department took all that and made it tough and simple-sounding:

If I liked femininity, I wouldn't be gay. By now I have gotten used to my friends' camping. I just don't participate.

Eric took me a lot of places as part of my continuing education. He showed me "the block." The block is in a fashionable area, right by Boston Common, where a single guy leaning against a car, thumbing a ride, or just walking slowly is probably looking for you. Or he may be out earning a little spending money after school. If so, he may not even be gay, as such. Today's high school kids are a lot more sophisticated than they were just a few years ago. Many of them—the ones who drive cross country in VW campers and have long hair and smoke dope—simply are not inhibited by the traditional social taboos. If a guy wants to pay $5 or $25 to blow him—why not? It feels good, the guy is grateful, and it's bread.

Naturally, that reasoning would sit uneasily with most parents. I'm not sure I buy it myself. But if that is all the significance the boy places on the experience, what's wrong with his logic? Not every kid is going to grow up to be President or a doctor or lawyer. So if he has a good body and likes to get blown and plans a career as an auto mechanic—and thank God for auto mechanics—why not? Is the FBI going to investigate his early years before they give him a license to fix your Mustang?

Eric and I leaned against a parked car and watched circling cars slow down as they went by. He explained that most cities have "blocks" or similar cruisy places. He said you could either find the places by flying over the city in a helicopter just after the bars close and looking for the only traffic jam in town or by asking any gay resident of the city. There are no signs, but everyone knows.

While we were on the subject of finding places, Eric

showed me his gay bar guide, available at most neighborhood pornographic bookstores. It listed the gay bars, restaurants, steam baths, and outdoor cruising spots, all over the world. Most bars (not Sporters) come and go so fast that even a fresh edition of any guide is outdated, but at the very least you get phone numbers of several places which, though they may no longer be "in" spots, can easily direct you to the kind of place you are looking for. Leafing through my own book, I see two places in Fort Smith, Arkansas, one in Alexandria, Louisiana, four in Blackpool, England, six in Tampa, eighteen in Atlantic City, seventy-two in Paris, two in Varna, Bulgaria, four in Butte, Montana, and one hundred twenty-five in San Francisco. Generally, even in a large city, there are only a few popular places at any given time. In Washington, for example, which has about thirty listings in the book, almost all the young people at the time of this writing go to the Lost and Found or to Pier 9. Everyone wants to be where everyone else is. The in spots shift frequently because everyone tends to be dissatisfied with everyone else and to think the grass just might be greener across town. (And because the police periodically bust gay bars, for one reason or another.) I would guess that the four bars in Butte, Montana, or even the one that is popular today, are not likely to be much to shout about, even on Saturday night. Still, if they are listed, there must be something going on. The same holds for those places the guide lists and labels "mixed." Granted, *any* place I have ever been has been "mixed," just by virtue of my gay presence. However, these mixed places would presumably not be listed if there weren't a fair amount of gay activity.

Eric and I didn't go to Sporters much. He knew that the more often I went, the faster I would find someone else. But we did go to a couple of other bars, just to see what they would be like.

Bars vary over at least three dimensions, the first being popularity. Next is age. No one stands at the door of younger bars turning away the over-thirty-five set (except in California, where they have some "under-twenty-one" bars); but few older men want to go where they will feel unwelcome. And then there is what you might call a bar's "degree of masculinity."

Eric and I went to the opening night of 1270, a new bar in town with a dance floor. Most young gay people dance, but Sporters doesn't have a dance floor. The new bar was jammed. Everyone wanted to see what kind of person would go there, what kind of bar it would turn out to be. That, of course, distorted things for a while. Really, 1270 could have taken on any of a number of personalities.

The new bar developed into a young, unpopular-except-on-weekends, largely black dancing bar. And nellie. Most of the clientele tend to be effeminate, to wear unbelievable costumes, and to dance extremely well. You would notice the people walking toward that bar. (Later the bar was remodeled and expanded, and its character changed.)

Sporters is in the middle on the masculinity scale, attracting, with many exceptions, the kind of people you wouldn't be likely to notice on the street as they walked by in jeans and flannel sport shirts.

Eric and I also took a look into the Shed, a leather bar in a rough section of town, at the other end of the masculinity scale. The Shed caters to the sadomasochistic client who arrives in a black leather jacket, stomping boots, maybe a white T-shirt stretched over too many muscles, a chain or two or some spikes on the wide leather belt—all this revving up to the bar on the biggest, loudest bike you have ever seen and, like as not, dying to find someone even tougher who will do the honors of rolling him over on his stomach and (all this back home, in privacy, of course) fucking him. With a mace, maybe.

I am drawing a caricature, I suppose. Few of the Shed's customers are so noticeable. For that you have to go to one of the leather bars in New York. New York has everything every other city has, squared. At one of these bars on the New York waterfront, with fake skeletons hanging from the ceiling and other cheery appurtenances, there is a sign on the door that says: "No Sneakers, Sandals, Slacks, Coats or Ties. Leather or Denim Only." Another featured fist-fucking shows.

Neither Eric nor I liked the largely older, largely unhappy-looking crowd of motorcyclists and cowboys at the Shed. *Were* they unhappy-looking, or did I just think they should be? Or am I just putting them down because I am embarrassed to acknowledge the part of me that likes this kind of rough scene? Hmmm? Actually, I guess it's just difficult to look happy and tough at the same time.

We went over to one other bar, the Other Side, which is run by the kind of people you wouldn't want to double-cross. (Sporters is not.) Most cities make it difficult for gay bars and baths to get licenses and to stay in business. In Boston you can't even open a place of worship, let alone a gay bar, without bribing officials up and down the line. But for the mob, they could be persuaded to make a little exception, maybe. How many licenses would you like? Fire inspections? Well, we would rather you didn't smoke in bed, sir.

Eric showed me around. We didn't go to "the baths," because Boston's gay life is too conservative to have good baths. There are two baths, but everyone knows that the good people don't ever go to them—so no one goes. Not only that, the idea of walking around in a towel looking for someone to have sex with takes more than a little getting used to, and in five years, Eric had not gotten used to it. That was fine by me.

Eric told me about lubricants, about crabs and the clap and syphilis; he told me, I hate to put it this way, many of the things I had always wanted to know about sex but had been afraid to ask. I say I hate to put it that way because I recently read the putrid chapter on homosexuality in that book, and I am thinking of filing a class-action suit on behalf of five or ten million homosexuals against Dr. Reuben, the author, who could not possibly have painted a more unfortunate, distorted and condescending picture.

Eric could have written a far more sensitive, accurate, helpful chapter. The only problem was, Eric was somehow devoid of any ambition and could barely move himself to turn over the phonograph record, let alone write a chapter on homosexuality. He was suffering from chronic unemployment, one symptom of which is lack of desire for a cure.

Eric could sense that I was beginning to get bored, that I was going out on my own more often, even though I still liked him a lot. We decided to spend a weekend in Provincetown, which, from what I had heard of it, promised to be anything but boring. Though unspoken, I think Eric and I both saw this as a nice way to end "our thing." In gay parlance, we hadn't been lovers those weeks; we had been "doing a thing."

CHAPTER 10

Provincetown, so much at the tip of the east-jutting Cape that it bends back westward toward Boston, toward California, is one of those places you always wondered about, where the highway finally ends. It doesn't interchange or intersect or angle sharply and slither down the coast. It just comes to the tippy-tip, sniffs the ocean in front and to either side, curls up in a tour of magnificent beaches, and spins you around a rotary and back on your way in the opposite direction—back east, actually, toward California, sort of. (You might say it goes both ways.)

Provincetown is a blustery barnacle in the winter with a small fishing population of Portuguese descent and a few hearth-warmed poets who perhaps find the bleakness "cosmic." In the summer, the Portuguese become hoteliers and restaurateurs; the poets become waiters and busboys. Young gays come from all over the country to be houseboys and poolside waiters. And Provincetown becomes a cotton-candy-apple carnival or a zoo, depending on your point of view. A resort town, a pickup town, an artist colony gone tourist trap, a sexual melting pot. Liberated. Liberating. Sick. A surfside Forty-second Street in the eyes of some, which, if it must exist at all, is best set at the geographical extremity; a model of lib-and-let-lib in the eyes of others, the nose of the map, not the tail.

There are straight people in Provincetown, Massachusetts. Hell, there is even "Provincetown High," as if this were any sort of place to raise kids! Many of the straight visitors in the summer are families and couples from other parts of the Cape, from Hyannis or Falmouth or Woods Hole, who would never dream of staying overnight in such a place.

The lifeguards are straight, but they only patrol the straight beaches—Race Point and the right side of Herring Cove. The *left* side of Herring Cove has the most crowded parking lot, but no lifeguards. If a lifeguard is a good-looking college boy in the process of finding himself, a summer of patrolling the left side of Herring Cove could rattle him. If he has become a lifeguard in order to flash his Plus-White-Plus smile at young lovelies on the beach, he would be disappointed by the left side of Herring Cove. There are some women on that side, but the most noticeable are built like sumo wrestlers, only with shorter hair, and tougher.

The Provincetown police force, one squad car eight months of the year, a regiment from mid-May to mid-September, is straight, a few latencies notwithstanding, and nervous. Last summer one of the policemen patrolling the dunes behind the left side of Herring Cove came upon a young man lying in the nude. Alone, no less. It is illegal to lie in the nude in the dunes of Provincetown, so this policeman *pulled his gun* and told the boy he was under arrest for nudity. "Try to run and I'll shoot." Gun drawn, he ordered the boy to put his skimpy swim suit back on and then marched him off to the police station, where he escaped with a $20 fine. Freud would have had a field day.

Yet there is a strange détente in Provincetown. Except for occasional sorties, like the dunes patrol just mentioned, the police don't bother anyone very much. Their salaries are paid out of tax money, and if the gay crowd left Provincetown, there would be no tax base. Loud music and dancing are illegal in Massachusetts on Sundays, so when the man at the Back Room door sees the police coming by to check, he waves to the discothèqueteer, who lifts the needle from the Stones and drops the other needle onto Johnny Mathis (well, almost), and 300 people stop dancing long enough for the men in blue to pop their heads in. It is a courteous arrangement.

The longtime Portuguese residents of the town seem to like their gay summer guests and neighbors, and not only because they are their bread and butter.

By and large, there is an understanding. Really, it is remarkable how there can be such an institution as "Provincetown" without anything in *writing*. We are so used to articles of incorporation, signs on doors, guidebooks, "colorful brochures." Provincetown is an understanding that is just passed on by word of mouth. Every year the benches in front of the Town Hall become the "meat rack." Every year the left side of Herring Cove is gay, the right side, straight. Of course, inevitably a straight family, either more naïve or more sophisticated than most, will walk left instead of right when they get to the beach. The first fifty yards or so are almost deserted, a sort of no-man's-land, with no lifeguard towers in sight. But if you keep walking, you quickly come to a thirty-yard layer of women tossing around footballs and cursing each other out. Maybe you should walk the other way? No? If not, you come to what must seem to an unsuspecting straight father, when his face finally flushes red with understanding, when he remembers how *his* father slapped him for having a gay high school teacher, when his memory flashes against his will to that never-mentioned night in sleep-away camp so many years ago . . . you come to what must seem to an unsuspecting straight father like mile upon mile of wildly camping queens swishing to the tape cassette tunes of *No, No, Nanette.* "Maybe we should walk down the other way, dear; I don't see any lifeguards here for the children."

A favorite Provincetown pastime, for both straight and gay, is to observe the people passing on the street and to try to type them by sexual orientation. I have to think that the gay players are better at this game than most of the straights. *Everyone* can pick out the stereotypes with a fairly high probability of being right. But the straight people miss a lot of less obvious signs that the gay people pick up like silver dollars. And then there are those people whose gayness is just not detectable. Unless you happen to see them dancing at one of the gay bars, that is.

The fact is, this trip to Provincetown with Eric was not my first. So, I suppose, before I tell you about who I met on this trip, I should go back and tell you who I didn't meet on the prior trip, some weeks earlier. The first time I came down, alone, I didn't meet anybody.

I didn't meet anybody because the kid at Sporters who gave me directions to P-Town told me only that Herring Cove was the gay beach. I had never been to a gay beach before and didn't know what to expect. I followed signs for Herring Cove, paid my dollar to park, and walked onto the beach. I naturally gravitated toward the lifeguards, who looked anything but gay and all the more attractive for that, and, though I walked a long way and saw a lot of different lifeguards all the way down the beach, which stretches forever, I didn't see anything particularly gay. I saw some kids without dates, some guys lying on blankets next to each other whom I would have been glad to get to know. But you don't just go up to two guys on the beach and introduce yourself! When I had run out of lifeguards to walk past, I walked a little farther until I ran out of people altogether. There is a limit to how far people will walk for a secluded piece of beach, and I had apparently reached that limit. I turned around and walked back. What the hell. I sat down near my favorite lifeguard and spent the afternoon alone on the beach, dozing, reading a crumpled, sweaty *Business Week*, going for an occasional swim.

I hadn't really come down to Provincetown for a good time anyway. I had had the makings of a fever when I left that morning; by the time I got back to Cambridge that evening my temperature was 102°. I had been feeling cosmic again, for the first time in a long while, and I wanted a change of scenery. Oh, cruel, cruel world which hast planned such torments for me! Et cetera, et cetera. You see, I had fallen in love, been led on—and dropped.

Or that's the way it had seemed at the time. I had gone with Eric to one of his gay student meetings at B.U., right there in the Student Union Building. With *signs* up for it and everything, and straight people you had to walk past in the reading lounge to get into the clearly labelled STUDENT HOMOPHILE LEAGUE meeting room. But my parents were 200 miles away, and I was, as I say, coming out with a vengeance. That evening I met a lot of young men, too many of whom struck me as the meek-bookwormy type who couldn't play baseball any better than I—nice guys, but nothing like my fantasies.

The "program" was 8-millimeter movies of the recent Student Homophile League outing to Crane's Beach; next week it would be a lady from the VD clinic to give us the lowdown. After the movies, I spotted one fellow out on the terrace talking to a few others. When I went for a closer look, I got a good firm handshake, a Southern accent, and a smile that was in between boyish and handsome. There is something about Southern accents—slow, easy, self-assured—that turns me on.

He was Freddie and hadn't seen me here before. I was me and hadn't been around very much. (By this time I knew I got points for being a newcomer.) He was from Atlanta, where he went to Georgia Tech, but was up here at Harvard summer school studying French. I wasn't really a student anymore, but was with my friend Eric—you know Eric? I had been to Yale, and I was just bumming around for the summer. (That image, I figured, would go over better than the IBM image.) He wanted to introduce me to his lover, who was over at the other end of the terrace.

His lover? Hmph. I was new to these things, but I knew enough to know that his lover posed a problem. On the other hand, I had the impression that those things didn't last very long, and when I met his lover, a thirtyish history professor type, the oldest one at the meeting, I knew that Freddie would surely drop him for me, the young, attractive Yalie.

("Lover" is a word that makes me squirm a little, but the only one available I know of. "Husband" or "wife," in the context of two guys, sounds even worse. "Best friend" is what I like—but it does not imply an exclusive, sexual, often cohabitational relationship.)

I didn't feel good about spoiling the professor's love affair, but I was sure he had had plenty of affairs before and would have plenty after. It was *my* turn. Eric was a fine friend, but Freddie was really "my type." I knew, because I got a hard-on when we shook hands, and it took a long time to go away. I was dying to go to bed with him. Here was a gay Brook-from-Tulsa. Here was the kid who would transfer from Georgia Tech to any of the myriad Boston schools, share my apartment in Cambridge, and share my life. Well, I'm not sure I thought much about his sharing my life. When I back off from the influence of a body like Freddie's and get my wits together, I realize that I am a rather independent, private person who is not awfully good at sharing things.

His lover was a nice enough guy, whom I made every effort to pretend to like. I was new at the game, but not new to being devious, and I caught on fast. I paid no attention to Freddie and talked and smiled only at his lover. I was all warmth and attention as I mentally jotted down the facts I needed: their last names and the hours Freddie's lover had to be at school. That way, I figured, I could find out their address and maybe just happen to bump into Freddie on the street when his lover was off at school. I was prepared to wait for days on that street, if necessary.

As it happened, it was not necessary. For one thing, Eric knew Freddie and his lover, their names and address. He told me they had been together for about a year. He warned me not to assume that just because Freddie's lover didn't strike *me* as particularly attractive that Freddie felt the same way. And he seemed upset that I would even consider interfering with the good relationship they had going. That would be unfair to both of them and selfish of me. I should just control myself.

I could understand that only in a mechanical, analytical sort of way. No one had ever tried to seduce a lover of mine, so I had no firsthand knowledge of what it would be like for Freddie's lover. Moreover, Freddie's unavailability made him all the more attractive to me. And, God damn it, I was prepared to be as selfish as I had to be: I *had* to become best friends with Freddie. Either Eric just didn't understand the strength of my need, or he was discouraging me out of his own self-interest. Yes! Eric didn't want me to be interested in Freddie; he wanted me to be interested in Eric. It took me a ridiculously long time to catch on to that. I was new to figuring out other people's feelings. Eventually, of course, I realized I had one of my red-white-and-blue striped U.S. Pro Court King Keds in my mouth (nine-and-a-half triple E), so I shut up and kept my thoughts about Freddie to myself.

The following Thursday Eric and I again went to the meeting, and Freddie was there. His lover had gone down to Washington to do some research in the National Archives and to spend the weekend with friends. Freddie wondered whether I wanted to drive out to the beach Saturday. Did I ever!

Saturday was wonderful and Freddie in the surf, with his red swim suit and brown glistening body—it really *was* Brook-from-Tulsa, and I was ecstatic. Unlike Eric, he was bursting with ideas and plans and stories of past accomplishments. Just the week before he had been on TV representing "The Youth of Today." And he was really interested in the things I had done at Yale and was doing for IBM. He wanted my advice on his future. It was a beautiful, complementary relationship. I was more experienced in the practical world; he was more experienced emotionally and sexually. He liked older, established people, and even at twenty-three I qualified. I liked younger guys who reminded me of those I had idolized at camp, in high school, in college. We really turned each other on.

We had fabulous sex that night. I thought so anyway. He said I hadn't seen anything yet—that he wasn't feeling all that well and so he didn't want to do much. Oh. Wait until next time, he said.

Speaking of next time, how about tomorrow night?

Freddie wasn't sure about Sunday night, because his lover would probably be coming back. He said he would call to let me know. Freddie didn't usually make it with other people, he told me, but he knew his lover would understand. Freddie had just wanted to do it with me and was happy that I wanted to become best friends.

Sunday he must have been too busy to call.

Monday I began to feel just a little gloomy.

When I hadn't heard from Freddie by Tuesday, I called him. His lover answered. Freddie was sick, he said. He had a fever and something wrong with his mouth. When Freddie woke up, he would give him the message. (Would he, really? I wondered.)

He didn't call me back Tuesday. He didn't call me back Wednesday. What was he, in a coma? How could he *do* this to me? I *knew* he liked me. He had to know how important he was to me. And now it was as if he had forgotten that I existed.

Thursday I decided to sit by the phone no longer. I got

in my car and headed for Provincetown, punching the buttons of my car radio any time a happy song came on, cosmic as I ever had been, and none the worse at it for my lack of recent practice. Color this page cosmic black. Black on black, easy on the eyes.

By Thursday evening I was light-headed and my gums felt as though my wisdom teeth were parading around my mouth. But I was not too light-headed to stop by B.U. on my way home from the elusive gay beach to see whether Freddie had bothered—the very least he could do, even if accompanied by his lover—to come to the meeting. I ascribed my light head to the long day in the sun and the driving. As for my wisdom teeth, they do occasionally make trouble. Mainly, I was thinking what I should say to Freddie when I saw him at the meeting.

He wasn't there, he hadn't been there, and, according to someone who knew him, he and his lover had gone down to Washington for another long weekend. Without so much as calling me to say good-bye!

Friday I was in bed with a temperature and what was either a mouthful of wisdom teeth or the same virus Freddie had. I must have caught it from him. (Germs! See? I knew it all the time!) That was delicious, cosmic-wise. Not only was I despicably wronged, I was now felled by grief and some mysterious, unidentified virus which would no doubt kill me by the time Freddie bothered to return my call and tell me what it was.

By Monday afternoon I knew Freddie had to be back, because he was not the type to miss classes, and yet he had not called. How was it possible? Telling my wounded pride that I was calling for medical reasons rather than emotional ones—chicken noodle soup felt like barbed wire in my sore mouth—I called Freddie that evening to find out just what strange disease I had contracted and how to cure it. This time I got him. Oh, *hi*! He apologized for not having called me back on Sunday or after I had called Tuesday; but he was feeling really rotten, and then there was no answer at my place on Thursday, and then they went down to Washington. How had I been? Oh, no! He was terribly sorry to hear I had caught his virus. I should just drink fluids and take aspirin. It took about a week to wind itself down, he said. I should feel fine by Thursday, but he felt terrible that I was sick.

That's all. No big deal. He had tried to call when he felt better, but I was away. Sure, he liked me. Sure, he wanted to get together. But I began to understand that he did love his lover and that I was just another friend he was glad he had met. Maybe even very glad—but for crying out loud, keep things in perspective.

I still felt bad that I wasn't the biggest deal in Freddie's life but I felt better. At least we would be good friends. At least the virus had only a couple more days to run.

Right on schedule, the virus vanished. Freddie called to see if I was better and invited me over to their place for a solid meal. That evening I got to know Freddie's lover, Cap. Cap knew enough about relationships to know there was no point trying to keep Freddie locked up, and it was fine with him if we wanted to pal around, he said. I stopped pretending I liked him, and liked him.

Freddie was my first gay "love," and I went into the brief episode defenseless. I had developed defenses for lots of things, but I was new to trying to develop love relationships.

I had loved straight people before, but I had not expected them to love me back and had not been hurt when they didn't. It was pure Ricky Nelson, aged sixteen, in love for the first time on *Ozzie and Harriet*.

Eric and I went down to Provincetown, and this time I was steered to the left as we walked onto the beach.

I had gotten used to heads turning when I passed in the bar. Well, to be honest, I enjoyed the ego boost. Even if there happened to be no one of great interest in the bar, it was still worth driving down there just to reaffirm my own "power." Having for so many years lived in the shadow of truly charismatic campers and collegians, the looks I got as I walked around the bar were like electric impulses charging my ego battery. I could even afford to attach my cables to some other ego I was not sure operated on the same current, to see if I could get something started, because if I failed, my battery would still have enough juice left over to start my own engine going around the bar again while I recharged.

Discovering the gay beach was rather like discovering high-voltage wires. The wiring at Sporters is a fine power source, but the Herring Cove cables were more powerful in direct proportion to the degree by which my body is more attractive than my face. (Such poetic metaphors, right?) I've got one of those faces that is on the border line. If I am happy and smiling, sort of radiating, and if I am tanned and well rested and zit-free, and my hair happens to be at the high point in its cycle between washings, not too wispy and not too greasy, then I am pleased with my face. As long as I don't think about it. If I start thinking about it and looking at it in the mirror, then I get self-conscious, and the radiance and the smile go, and I get more self-conscious and may as well call it a night.

My body, on the other hand, is much more reliable. I suppose I owe it to all those sports in high school and to general good fortune in my bone structure. I don't work out with weights or anything. We have an understanding: I don't try to change it or elongate it or tax it greatly; it looks good when I take my clothes off. A little on the short side next to some of my friends, but well proportioned and well defined. It's a tennis-player-in-alligator-shirt kind of body.

Eric just lay on his Budweiser beach towel and soaked in the August sun. I walked around the beach, swam a lot, discovered friends I had met in Sporters, and met their friends. When we first arrived, the beach was perhaps forty yards wide, between the lapping ocean and the ridge of sand that hid the hot dry dunes beyond. People were scattered widely. But as the tide came in, everyone got friendlier, some more stoned, some more drunk, and the ocean snipped away at our ribbon of beach, leaving us finally with about five yards between water and ridge. Perhaps that's what pushed some pairs into the dunes; but Eric told me it was more likely they wanted some privacy while they fucked. Oh.

The "in" bar that summer was Piggy's, on Shank Painter Road. It was particularly nice because the locals went there, some straight, some gay, and there was a warm Portuguese atmosphere. Well, I'm guessing Portuguese; the closest I've been to Portugal is Tossa. But whatever it was seemed genuine and comfortable rather than consciously designed for effect. Piggy's seemed to have been discovered rather than promoted. You didn't recognize much of the music they played (a pleasant change), but it made you want to dance and get into the rhythm of the place.

For most of the summer I had refused to dance when I was at a bar or a party, or even at a gay lib dance. Cowboys don't dance. How could guys dance with other guys? (Massachusetts did not allow people of the same sex to touch each other when they dance—tolerance has its limits.)

As time went on, I realized it was a little foolish to stand on the edge of a dance floor bouncing up and down in time to the music, wanting to dance, but fearing that it would somehow make me less a man. Just dance in a manly way, and you will have the best of both worlds. There is a limit to the degree to which you have to feel superior to everyone else, you know. I mean, you *are* gay, after all. I mean, we understand that it will take you a while to get used to everything, to lower your inhibitions, to accept your new life. But you are not going to be "just come out last month" all your life, friend. So have a drink, relax, and enjoy it. People wouldn't have been dancing throughout recorded history if there weren't something to it. By August of my twenty-third year I finally began to enjoy dancing, a little.

Piggy's was jammed with attractive people that night. There were weekenders from Boston and New York and summer residents, many of them waiters and busboys, who came over to Piggy's when they got off their jobs around eleven o'clock.

Who is that tall blond boy, Golden Boy, over by the bar? He was surrounded by others. Usually, when I walk closer to a potential fantasy, reality comes into focus. But not this time. Was it possible that someone that good-looking could be gay? Could be real, even? What I wouldn't give to be six five and blond with a perfect Ryan O'Neal face like that and the same self-assurance. *There* is a kid who has the world around his finger.

Eric told me he was Mike York, going into his last year of college, and president of his class, if he remembered right. Undoubtedly! Oh, how I envy people who have it made before they start. I take for granted my good fortune and envy those who are born even more fortunate. Here was John Tunney–John Lindsay–John Kennedy, aged twenty-one.

Eric managed to introduce us later in the evening, but Golden Boy wasn't paying much attention. He was on his way out with someone else. Hello, how are *you?* he asked like a politician, looking at the top of my brown-haired head and then moving on to other well-wishers. Wow.

I spent the rest of the evening thinking about Golden Boy, wishing I were able, as he was, to point at anyone I wanted, flash my perfect smile, and go off with my instant conquest to Wyoming or the Portuguese Y.

I badgered Eric to tell me who everyone else was too— particularly the people I had seen talking with Golden Boy. If I could make friends with his friends, maybe I could elbow my way into his circle. The best looking of Golden Boy's friends, in an objective sort of way—handsome, very handsome, but not sexy-looking, not blond—was Chris. Another Southern accent—Montgomery, Alabama—and affable. He didn't stay long either. Someone asked him to dance, and Eric and I resumed our conversation. Eric thought Chris was better looking than Golden Boy, he said. Eric had done a thing with Chris when Chris was first coming out, the summer before me. Chris is a nice guy, Eric said—a little wistfully, I thought. He's down here for the summer working as a waiter in Wellfleet at some spiffy lobster place. He starts Harvard Business School in a few weeks.

Yeah, okay, but tell me about Golden Boy, for crying out loud. Who wants Harvard Business School? Golden Boy is going to be a senior in *college*. Do you know what the word "college" does to me?

The next day I saw Golden Boy on the beach, surrounded, of course. I walked by his circle a couple of times; no one noticed. Again. No one noticed. Then I went for a long swim and timed it so that I came slushing healthily, glisteningly out of the water right down from where Golden Boy was lying in the sun. You know how you come out of salt water, having a hard time at first keeping your balance after the motion of the waves, eyes shut tight as you rub the salt water from your face—apparently just staggering uphill without really seeing where you're going. You aren't thinking about the impression you're making or where you're going, you're just trying to get the water out of your ears and the hair out of your eyes—and you know damn well you look as appealing as you'll ever look, perhaps because you know it looks as though you're not trying to look appealing. Paying no attention to where I was going, the first people I "happened" to notice as my eyes finally were willing to stay open—were Golden Boy and his group. "Say, how's it goin'?" I asked casually, feigning moderate surprise, the way you are allowed to when you have stumbled out of the water and happen to recover your equilibrium next to someone you recognize. "It's Mike, isn't it?" I asked, as though trying to remember the name of someone I had met before who had made a mild impression on me.

Golden boys apparently have egos, too. He smiled at being recognized. Before I could be shot down with an "I can't remember your name," I said, "John. I met you with Eric last night at Piggy's." Sure, I remember, lied the class president.

I had learned enough about the game in those three months of being out to know not to press it any further. If I looked more than casually interested, my chances, slim as they were, would be shot. However, if I looked as though I could live without Golden Boy, I would be set apart from the crowd. I might be noticed. I didn't look for an open space on their blanket. I just resumed my wet stumbling in the direction of my own blanket, heart pounding, to talk over this great new development with Eric.

Eric was not enjoying the weekend. It was supposed to be *our* weekend, but I couldn't control myself. I was immature; he was grumpy. I thought of staying an extra day, but Eric said he had to get back to Boston, so we left. I knew I would be back the following weekend, the last weekend in August.

CHAPTER 11

My Summer of '42, if you will allow me to be sentimental, was almost over. It had been a wonderful, exciting, full summer. Even the week when I was recovering from Freddie had been a good week, thinking back on it, because it was so human.

For the longest time, when I was growing up, I actually thought I had somehow been born without feelings. I mean I consciously thought about that in high school, wondering whether it was some sort of biological phenomenon, or somehow related to my Big Secret, or what. When my father's mother died of lung cancer, I was nine. She had always been good to me, a wonderful woman, but having to visit her at her sickbed was an imposition I resented. I tried to feel sympathetic, but I felt put upon. After she passed away, my parents were in tears, on and off, for days. I had never seen my father cry before. I knew I should feel bad, but I didn't really. At the funeral I felt itchy because of the wool suit I was made to wear.

That same year my elementary school teacher had to be out almost all spring because of what she claimed was an appendectomy, but was apparently something far more serious. From nine to two every day she had supported my position as the best little boy in the class. She was the kind of teacher who genuinely loved her children. But while we were drawing get-well cards for her, I was feeling sorry for myself: All that work to get the best grades in the class was now in jeopardy, with a new substitute teacher who might not count all my goodness from the months before she showed up.

I certainly didn't hate my mother or father, but I couldn't detect any great love for them, either. I was oddly neutral, feelingless. As for Goliath, he could go jump in the lake. And Sam? Sam had kinky hair, and when he was dog-napped, I was the only one in the family who had to *pretend* to feel bad about it.

I didn't see anything so special about the Mona Lisa. Poetry left me totally blank, bored. I did not react to love songs that should have made me sad. I had feeling for one thing and for one thing only: me. I felt guilty about that, considering the fact that I was supposed to be so good. As I said in the first chapter, it made me feel phony. It also made me feel "different."

As I got older, I seemed to develop some feelings, if not my full share. Our new dog was much more lovable than Sam had been, in my view, and when he finally had to be put to sleep, I was genuinely sad to hear about it. I was at Yale by then. But the Mona Lisa and the poems and the love songs still left me cold, coldly analytical, calculatingly self-centered, even at Yale. As I rose in my teens, I just gradually stopped worrying about my lack of feelings. I learned the word "hypocrisy" and wondered whether I was the only one who pretended to like the Mona Lisa. I saw a movie about a soldier whose buddy was killed in the foxhole next to him, and how that soldier felt *glad* when it happened. He hated himself so much for feeling glad that his legs became paralyzed, psychosomatically, until a doctor years later told him it was *natural* to feel glad—not glad that your buddy had been hit, but that it hadn't been you. When the soldier heard that, he regained use of his legs. It's *natural* to be selfish. All in all, I decided, I probably had fewer feelings than most people, but that was the least of my problems. It was a lot easier to pretend I liked the Mona Lisa than to pretend I liked Hilda Goldbaum, let me tell you.

Now I had had my Summer of '42. Now, crushed by Freddie, it was apparent that I was as feeling as anyone else. Sad as it had been, it was a relief to know the songs were written for me, too. I was no longer left out of the stream of common experience, no longer the superfluous man.

I had been dashing around like crazy that summer, spending virtually every night at the bar, or else at a Student Homophile meeting and the bar afterward, and having sex with loads of different people.

Of all the people I had met that summer, Eric and Freddie and Golden Boy were the only three I would remember for long. Yet Eric never *did* anything and couldn't keep me interested, nice a guy as he was; Freddie loved Cap; and GB, well, GB would give me something to think about during the fall. I would shortly be back at work, running a feasibility study for some government work IBM might wind up doing. But I knew that I would not be working the kind of single-minded eighty-hour weeks I had right out of Yale, at least not for quite a while. I was determined to make up for the living I had missed. And I had to come to terms with such questions as: Who would I come home to when I was fifty, or even thirty, and no longer riding near the top of the gay world? In fact, who would I

come home to tomorrow? Did I want to come home to anyone, or to bring someone new home every night?

I was learning that I had some basic characteristics that
would stand in the way of long-term relationships. The kind
of guy who would turn me on sexually, I thought, would not
be the kind I could have for a lover. He would be all the
things I wanted to be when I was growing up: cool and
dumb, mainly. A young, dumb, trashy truck driver with a
tight, smooth, rock-hard but not grotesquely muscled body,
whose only pastimes were getting stoned, listening to rock,
and letting people dig his body. Too dumb to have anything
to say; too cool to get enthusiastic except for an occasional
"Wow, man, are you ready for this shit?" as he smoked; and
too trashy to be seen with. Great fantasy material in a mas-
ochistic sort of way. Though again I find it hard to write
about, I suppose part of me wants someone like that to pin
me to the wrestling mat, to dominate me, to hate me for being such a goody-goody and ridicule me for being so out of
it—even to do the unmentionable to me.

Clearly, it would be difficult to form a good long-term relationship with a cool, trashy young kid whom I wanted to
have humiliate me.

That all fits neatly into the "homosexual self-hate" chapter of psychoanalysis. Yet I don't believe it really does fit.
I'm not sure that feelings like that are by any means exclu-
sively gay. And I *know* I don't really hate myself. If I believe,
as I obviously do, that I'm about the neatest thing since in-
tegrated circuits, is it meaningful for someone else to come
along and look at my file and say, "Well, no, I am sorry to
inform you that, really, you are not happy with yourself as
you seem to have convinced yourself you are. Actually, you

do hate yourself—so much that you can't stand to admit it. For forty-five dollars an hour for the rest of your life, I will gladly try to help you face up to the fact. Perhaps if we can get you that far, we can even get to the root of your unconscious unhappiness and build you all over again a true happiness."

Then there is the other side of me, probably the larger half. I am aggressive, egotistical, competitive, and dominating, as I hold my trick down in a half nelson, one arm tightly around his waist so he can't struggle, and hoping, frankly, that he will struggle while I ram into him and feel my muscles flexing and tensing, in complete control of him, and then, finally sweating, panting, shoot into his helpless body.

So you see, it works both ways with me, as I guess it does with many people, straight or gay.

Beyond the fact that many of the people who turned me on most were not likely to be the kind I would want to share a home with, there was the problem that roles, in and out of bed, are more easily assigned between a dominating man and a submissive woman than between two men, though perhaps this is changing with the women's liberation movement. (Uneasy as I admittedly am with women where sex is involved, on a rational level I am, of course, all for them. One of my closest friends is a straight woman. Gloria Steinem is my hero.)

And yet another obstacle seemed to stand in the way of my forming a lover relationship. I seemed to have been conditioned to fall for the kind of guy who wouldn't fall for me in return. I was turned on as long as someone was, for whatever reason, unattainable; but as soon as he showed affection for me or—God forbid!—needed me more than I needed him, I knew he wasn't truly Brian or Tommy or Hank. I realized that part of this was simply the universal hard-to-get syndrome, part the anticipation-is-better-than-the-attainment syndrome. Yet it seemed to go further.

That has made truly satisfying, lose-yourself-in-it sex hard to come by, as you might imagine. It is tantamount to saying, "I don't *want* to have sex. Cowboys *don't* kiss, cowboys have fistfights." Yet my body wants to have sex; it wants to be touched and tickled and rubbed and hugged and kneaded and warmed. And I am not about to have fistfights, because pain hurts. Not in fantasies it doesn't; it's fine in fantasies. But it provides no pleasure whatever in fact. It hurts. I've checked.

This being the case, I simply grin at the idea of having truly superb sex night after night with the same guy. Sure, I would like it to happen, and I will welcome the gradual lowering of some of these obstacles, should they start to lower with time.* But the last thing I am going to do is let myself take them too seriously, let them make me unhappy, dedicate my life to what may well be the impossible task of changing around what appears to be the core of my sexuality. I can remember having had some of these feelings, some of the same fantasies nearly twenty years ago, when I was five! This is *me*, Great Scorekeeper, and I have learned to love it. If it changes, fine; when it does, I will love the changes, too.

Anyway, I had come to know more about myself that summer, and I had decided quite definitely that there was noth-

*They have.

ing "wrong" with the way I was, nothing to feel guilty about. I was tired of feeling guilty, and I was just a little pissed off that society had made me feel guilty so long.

I began to feel indignant, instead. And I began to feel as though I wanted to change things if I could. I acknowledged that there were other more pressing world problems than the social stigma of homosexuality, but this happened to be the "cause" I was most interested in.

Yet what could I do without making my parents miserable? What if they saw me on TV marching for gay lib? Lots of gay kids either have no parents or hate them. I have them and love them. My mother would understand, I think, if I told her. My father would, too; only it would be much harder. Men find male homosexuality harder to accept than women. It is more threatening; they have been trained to find it repulsive. No doubt my father would feel he had not projected the proper image for me to identify with. Nonsense. Look at Goliath. As normal and heterosexual a giant as you would ever find. Yet how can my father be expected to be objective about a thing like this?

As for all the employers who would regretfully pass up my résumé if I were openly gay, and black résumés, and women's résumés—fuck 'em. There are already too many career choices for the average college graduate to choose between. A little discrimination would just narrow things down conveniently. My present boss does know I am gay, does know about the book. I wanted it that way, because I am spoiled now: I have told all my straight friends I am gay, I have told Goliath and Goliath-in-Law, and the only people for whom I am willing to keep my guard up are my parents. Now, you may surely say that I have no more business telling my boss I am gay than you have telling yours you are straight. That's a private matter. No one should care who you sleep with.

Exactly! When the unlikely day comes that no one *does* care that I sleep with guys, there will indeed be nothing to tell anyone about.

Feeling self-righteous this way and feeling so happy about the whole summer, I decided to tell my parents everything.

I drove down to Brewster to spend a weekend with them and went over and over my speech as I drove. Naturally, I would have to check that no company had been invited over for that night or Sunday; I would have to get a couple of drinks down my father. Mainly, I would have to somehow impress upon him the importance of keeping his mouth shut until I had said all I wanted to say. My father is no less impatient than I am, and after my first sentence he would be interrupting, telling me to get to the point. Well, to be understood properly, it just couldn't all be said in a sentence. So *please*, trust me and listen:

"I have some good news that will take you a little getting used to, but I very much want you to share it with me. Why don't you sit—"

"You're getting married!" my father would say.

"Oh, dear, who *is* she? Why haven't you told us about her before!" my mother would say.

"*Wait!* It's not what you think and you are absolutely going to have to just sit for ten minutes and hear me out, all of it, until I finish. *Please.*"

"All right, bun," my father would say to my mother, "let him get to the point."

"But *you* were the one who inter—"

"Mom, listen. For the longest time I had a problem. Do you remember how serious and sullen I always used to look when I came back from school? Well, I had a personal problem that bothered me for a long time. I would have told you all about it, only it was just not the kind of problem you could possibly have helped me work out, and I knew it would make you upset. The good news is that this summer I have worked things out. This has been a very happy summer for me, and I think the future is going to be very happy, and now that—"

"For crying out loud, will you come to the point!"

"—and now that I have solved it, I feel the only way we can really be close is if I share it with you. The reason I am taking so long to get to it is that it is quite complicated and it's going to be very hard for you to understand."

My parents are silent now, running through the worst fears they have ever had for their son, possibly considering this one, but, I would guess, probably not. Maybe—but I just don't think they would have allowed themselves to think such things about their son. They look worried, sympathetic, and they wish I would come to the point.

"Ever since I was eleven"—I am looking at the floor now to spare them (me) the embarrassment of having to show (see) their initial shock and, perhaps, revulsion, when I say it—none of this would be so bad if they didn't love me so much—"I have known that I liked boys instead of girls. You can imagine that that was an upsetting kind of thing to know, as I'm sure you feel upset now hearing about it"—I am talking very quickly now, not about to brook interruption—"but this summer I have come to terms with myself, and I am very happy."

"Oh, my God," says my father, who, for all his quickness

of wit, is still back where I said the part about having always liked boys instead of girls.

"Thank God," says my mother, crying, assuming that what I mean about having come to terms with myself is that I have finally started making it with chicks and that I have gotten myself on the right track.

"I forgot something in my preface. I forgot to say how I know that the one thing you want more than anything is for me to be happy—isn't it?"

"Of *course*," says my mother, responding to a very old sales technique: Get them committed to your position. Nod your head and smile; the prospect will nod her head and smile.

"Well, I know we will have to spend hours talking about it so you can understand why I am really happy, but—"

"Oh, my God," whispers my mother as she realizes that I *still* like boys instead of girls. She is flashing to what she did wrong, to how unhappy I must be, to statistics she has heard about psychiatric cures, to what my father must be thinking.

My father is flashing to what his father did to him when he heard he had a gay teacher, to swishy types who had occasionally approached him in his youth, to fleeting images of unthinkable sexual perversions which are instantly pushed from his mind, but which keep fleeting, flitting back, to what he did wrong, to what my mother must be thinking.

The trick, I know, would be to keep talking and make them listen, not let them think. "I know we have to spend a lot of time talking about it, but if what you really want is for me to be happy, I know you will come to understand it and be happy for me."

And on we would no doubt go for some time, my recounting many of the stories now recounted here, my naming all the famous, important, wholesome citizens I could possibly think of, all the way from Alexander the Great and Leonardo da Vinci to the present, who I knew were gay, so they would have lots of new images to identify their son with, not just the effeminate types that even people as naïve and wholesome as my parents recognize on the street and consider, *a priori*, "pathetic."

And, I think, because my parents are awfully bright and loving and because there really *is* nothing to be ashamed of, they could gradually come to accept it, more or less. Probably, my father would simply never want to talk about it. My mother might even become rather enthusiastic, with time, though always expecting me to see the light one day and pop off a few grandchildren.

Lots of my friends have told their parents and have either formed a tacit agreement that it is okay but not to be talked about and we love you no matter what you do, or else have a real, genuine, talking acceptance of the whole thing. More power to them.

Unfortunately, far more of my friends would never dream of telling straight friends, let alone their parents. Many of those who have tell horror stories. Jon Martin (of course I met him in a bar after I came out; all was forgiven) told me about one of our Yale classmates whose parents were told by a third party that their son was gay (a hell of a thing for a third party to do, of course), and they never talked to him again. Disowned.

I knew that my parents would react relatively well. I could probably even keep them from sending me to an analyst three times a week, although that would be their first impulse: "If only you had told us! But no matter what it costs, we will cure you!"

And there is always the chance that I underestimate their savvy, which would be fine with me. I certainly have not tried much lately to put up a front, and I keep changing the subject, raised less frequently now, of who I'm dating. Views are changing fast, and they live in *New York*, for crying out loud. So maybe they have a very good idea what's going on but have not cared to acknowledge it or have their suspicions confirmed. Maybe.

Whichever scenario it would have been, I chickened out when I reached Brewster. I decided that telling them was almost certain to make them unhappy, and I doubted whether the new closeness and honesty in our relationship would be sufficient compensation for the hurt. Nor did I relish the idea that they might, conceivably, no longer look upon me as perfect. Well, how could they? Was I ready to live without their thinking I was perfect? Every week I call and tell them my latest accomplishments, and they say to themselves, and I hear it: "That's our boy—the best little boy in the world." Why shatter all that for them or for me?

In fact, to date, two happy years later, I haven't shattered it, but again I am drawing close. I told myself then that I would only tell them when there was reason to, when I thought there was a chance they might otherwise hear it first from someone else. Now with this book is that time, and I don't know what I will do.

How could I write a book that might cause my parents so much pain? I am writing it because I want to, because like everyone, I want to try to do something meaningful with my life, because I *do* want to be the BLBITW, and because I think they will understand.

Very heavy. For me anyway. But there was still a week left in my Summer of '42, and, as these things sometimes happen, the most important event of the summer was not to occur until that last weekend, the weekend after Eric and I went down to Provincetown, when I went back alone.

It didn't seem so all-fired important at the time. I can't even remember whether Golden Boy was around—I think he was and that I got in another "hello" or two, little investments in the relationship he didn't know I was building with him.

All that happened of significance that weekend is that as Piggy's was closing, having found no one to go home with—and home was an extravagant $20 motel room that I was loath to waste, not to speak of the blow to my ego of sleeping alone on a Saturday night in Provincetown—as I walked toward the door, I saw Chris, the Harvard Business School student Eric had introduced me to, one of Golden Boy's friends, looking a little drunk, a little dejected by the door. Not really my type, but better this than nothing.

"You're Chris, aren't you? Eric's friend?"

"Say, how's it goin'?"

"Not bad—you?"

"Oh, not too bad." (Harvard and Yale were in rare form.)

"Look, I'm staying down the street—would you like to come back with me?"

"Sure."

It would be nice to romanticize that first night together or the next day on the beach. Roberta Flack tears me apart when she sings about "the first time ever I saw your face." When I hear that song, I go misty immediately, and a cosmic—no, I think a genuinely painful—expression washes across my face. When I hear that song, I immediately think of Chris, and tears well up in my eyes. The tears don't well up because I saw the sun rise in Chris's eyes that night. I didn't. They well up because I wish I *had* seen the sun rise in Chris's eyes, because I wish I were the kind of person to whom beautiful romantic things like that could happen, because I wish there were a way Chris and I, or maybe anyone and I, could really make it.

CHAPTER 12

Chris and I fell in love.

Well, Chris fell in love with me, and I sort of pushed myself in love with him.

That last weekend in August, just before I was to start work again, Chris and I left Piggy's together. In the morning, he said he knew a great beach in Truro, nearby. Most Eastern beaches run into water on one side and asphalt parking lots on the other. This beach had the water, of course, but instead of the parking lot, this beach ran into a hundred-foot sand cliff. The cliff was so nearly vertical that you could bound down in exuberant free-fall ten-foot moon leaps, forming steep right triangles as you went: Left leg pushes out two feet from the cliff, fall eight feet, right foot rejoins the hypotenuse. Down you bound, a dozen steps to the beach below. There was also something nice about its not being a "gay" beach. Chris had been out longer than I had, for just over a year, and he may have had his fill of gay beaches.

I was excited about making friends with someone who would be in Boston in the fall, whom I wouldn't feel embarrassed to introduce to Hank and Brook. Chris was starting out at Harvard *Business* School, for crying out loud. We could "re*late*" to each other.

Chris's job was ending the following week, just as mine would be beginning. He would be moving into Chase Hall at Harvard Business School, a mile's walk from my apartment in Cambridge. Very convenient. We agreed to get together back in Boston.

As it happened, we spent almost every evening together that fall. Although my new responsibilities at work kept me occupied, we generally talked on the phone once a day, or even twice, and I never stayed at the office past six or seven or on weekends the way I had before coming out.

After a few weeks we came to the realization that we were not just "doing a thing." We were "lovers." Two gay men who spend most of their time together and who are supposed to feel guilty if they have sex with someone else are lovers. That was, after all, the object of the game I had been playing for three months. That was the point of going to the bar night after night, looking. To the gay bar or, I suppose for that matter, to the straight dating bar. That was what all the movies and the songs were about, and I was ready to get in on the fun. Enough of humming "What Kind of Fool Am I?" It was about time I had a lover, particularly inasmuch as I wouldn't have much time, now that work had started again, to go around looking. I am very practical about these things, as you can see.

What I am saying is that Chris was my lover because he fell in love with me; I was his lover because I liked him a lot and wanted to "have a lover."

One of the reasons we managed to stay together as long as we did, from September to April, is that he loved me in a strong, silent sort of way. He didn't tell me over and over that he loved me or bring me gifts or anything. If he had been effusive or had tried to make me more affectionate or had told me the true extent to which my looking at other people hurt his feelings, he would have turned me off.

We were not 100 percent sexually compatible. I couldn't fulfill my cowboy fantasies with him. Playing out fantasies is childish and embarrassing, and if you are embarrassed, you can't get into it. So when we had sex, quite frequently at first, I would just shut my eyes and fantasize. Compatibility, I think, is in some part measured by the ability of the partners to climax at the same time. Well, I could never do that with Chris (or anyone else) because that kind of precision timing required an awareness of the other person; I was concentrating largely on my fantasies in order to be able to come. So any orgasmic simultaneity became the full responsibility of my partner. Go ahead and come when I come, that's okay by me; only don't make too much noise or move around too much, or you will make me lose my train of thought, and *I* won't be able to come. And if it's all the same to you, try not to get it on me.

I was apologetic about all this, and Chris was understanding. We got to know each other awfully well, and I managed to tell him about my squeamishness and weaknesses and insecurities. I even managed to force myself to describe those famous fantasies in some lurid detail, embarrassing as they were to own up to. Telling him did not improve our sex, but it made him the undisputed closest friend I had—I mean *no one* had gotten that far into my head—and he was willing to put up with my inhibitions and hangups.

One thing we tried was putting Smucker's old-fashioned raspberry jam, my absolute favorite, all over Chris's cock. Like grinding up a child's medicine in a bowl of Jell-O. Very

Skinnerian. It took me several months to reacquire my taste for Smucker's raspberry jam.

Our sex wasn't sufficiently satisfying for either of us, so we decided, as some gay lovers do, to go out on our own and do it with other people every so often. Two rules: Always tell you did it (after the fact), and never do it with someone we both really care about. Telling assured each of us that we really knew what was going on. Telling after the fact was the least painful way: "Chris, I did it with some trashy number from the bar, but there was nothing to it. I got him out of my system. You're still my main man." That was all there was to it, although I guess Chris didn't like my doing it with other people, even though we had agreed. Rule two was touchy. We wouldn't do it with each other's friends, because that could get very painful and complicated. But it required considerable self-restraint, inasmuch as we both tended to have attractive friends. Well, Golden Boy for example.

Golden Boy and Chris were very close. I don't know why they had never had sex—their relationship just never developed that way. But they spent so much time together that lots of people at the bar thought they were lovers.

I got to see a lot of Golden Boy, and we became friends. The three of us would often go do things together, although three can be an uncomfortable number. Even where sex isn't involved, someone usually feels left out. My freshman year at Yale I had a second roommate besides Roger-with-the-Kleenex-by-his-bed-every-morning, but he was so left out I even forgot to mention him earlier. Well, if it's bad with three "straight" freshmen, it's much worse when there are little streaks of love and envy and jealousy and whatnot flashing around the room. Chris wanted Golden Boy and me to be friendly, but not too friendly. I felt left out when they started talking about things they had done together before I had appeared on the scene. I didn't like it when people thought Golden Boy was Chris's lover—not because I loved Chris so much, but because it wounded my pride and made me feel all the more left out. And I was jealous of Chris's relationship with Golden Boy.

This area of friends can get quite sticky, more so in gay life than straight, because two gay lovers are likely to be attracted by a third gay guy, where with a straight couple, only the girl would be attracted by another guy and only the guy would be attracted by another girl. The two lovers naturally find themselves competing for the third party. Maybe not competing to get into bed with the third party. Maybe just competing for the biggest smile and the warmest handshake on parting. Egos are involved. Naturally, a gay lover relationship based on love, not looks, holds up under the strain—and many do. But it's a strain nonetheless.

Not only are there more combinations and permutations of emotion in gay life, because everyone can be attracted by everyone else, but there are also fewer restrictions imposed by society to help you avoid temptation. Far from being a sacred institution in society, it is illegal for two men to marry. Thus there is no legal affirmation of a lover relationship, no crowd of well-wishers to witness the ceremony, no kids, natural or adopted, to bind the marriage. You are already outside the moral code, so you can forget about "doing the right thing for appearance's sake." Moreover, being outside the moral code, you don't have its discipline to help you order your life and to help you cope with temptation. Certainly, one can form his own moral code and be true to himself. But creating one's own—and sticking to it—is harder than conforming to preexisting, pervasive social norms.

Other problems gays have remaining faithful to their lovers are: The career problem, which is beginning to appear in straight life also with the feminist movement. How will gay lovers stay together if their careers conflict geographically? And the dominance problem. Who will do the dishes if both guys happen to be rather aggressive and masculine and unwilling to take on the "feminine role," circa 1955?

Three is a complicated number. Seven is ludicrous, but wait.

Golden Boy was hopelessly hung up on a young attorney named Dennis Moyer. Dennis had recently graduated from Harvard Law School and worked for one of Boston's stodgier firms, in the corporate taxation department. I was surprised when I first met him at Sporters. Here was Golden Boy, who could have had anyone he wanted, choosing a decent but unspectacular-looking guy in his late twenties. Now I know there is much more to life than looks, but in gay life most of the people you meet you meet on the basis of their looks, and you find out what's inside them only later.

As I got to know Dennis and as I got to know Golden Boy better, I began to understand. Dennis appears to be stability personified. He smokes a pipe; he speaks in carefully considered, deep tones. He is solid and masculine. Someone to lean on. Someone to complement a less stable personality. Dennis is the mature breadwinner type. Golden Boy, I learned first to my instinctive dismay and now to my amusement, likes to keep house.

I was startled to realize that Golden Boy, who had the

world around his finger, was not as happy as I was—I who didn't even enjoy kissing. Golden Boy was handsome; Golden Boy had no hangups in bed; Golden Boy was president of his class; and Golden Boy was in the depths of despair over Dennis Moyer.

If that sounds a mite melodramatic, it's the way GB would want it. I think he is a little like me in the way he enjoys his cosmic depression. He is a romantic and was determined that his woe-begotten relationship with Dennis should be the world's saddest love story.

Whenever Chris and I saw GB, we heard another episode. I never heard them from Dennis's end, so I can't say exactly who was being cruel to whom, who was being unfair. All I know is that Dennis was an all-consuming passion for GB.

One day, after GB and I had become rather close friends, he called me (I think Chris was not in at the time, or else he would have called Chris first) and announced, after I asked him why he sounded so terrible, that he had tried to kill himself the night before. He had just given up on life. If he couldn't have things work out with Dennis—and he couldn't—then he had no reason to go on living.

You *what?*

Well, he had swallowed a whole bottle full of sleeping pills up on the fourth floor of the library around midnight, in one of those rooms that was *sure* to be deserted until morning. He would have done it back at the dorm, but, of course, he might have been discovered—and, even if not, he wanted to spare his neighbors the horror of finding his corpse. So he went up to that deserted room and, naturally, fell asleep. But apparently some girl he knew went up there to study for an exam. She tried to wake him up, and then she tried harder, and then she got frightened and called the campus police and they called an ambulance and took him to Mass. General where the emergency staff pumped his stomach, and now he was home.

Can I reconstruct my feelings as Golden Boy described his attempted suicide? There was the pleasure you feel, but do not admit, when you hear another person's problems. You are instinctively glad that *you* don't have that problem—that it's your buddy who was hit, not you, out there in that foxhole. And there is the excitement. You want the two-alarm blaze to be put out with a minimum of damage to the building—but part of you wants the flames to go spectacularly out of control escalating the blaze to a major five-alarm disaster. Then there is the feeling of superiority as someone lets down his guard and tells you his problems. There is pleasure in feeling superior to a Golden Boy. You may not be as good-looking, but you can cope, and that makes you feel good. Then, too, it was pleasurably flattering to be the first of Golden Boy's inner circle to hear this dreadful news. Hadn't I always wanted someone like him to need me? (Of course the very act of needing changed his image—made him seem weaker.) What could make us closer friends than sharing a secret like this? That thought was pleasing. It *was* a secret, of course. I love secrets. The only people who would know would be the girl who found him, the people at the hospital, me, Chris, and Dennis Moyer. (Well, what was the point of the suicide if you didn't let Dennis Moyer know about it?) And it appeared that I would be the first to tell Chris the awful news, as GB had been unable to reach him and I was meeting him later that day for dinner. Everyone sort of likes to be the bearer of important news, even bad news.

Understand, such selfish feelings can only be written with a red crayon. If the Great Scorekeeper ever got hold of them—well, I would just have to deny ever having felt them. Like you, I despise people who delight in the misfortunes of others—and I *loathe* people who delight in my own misfortunes. I know exactly what feelings an attempted suicide should evoke, and I either had them, too, or pretended I had them. Sometimes in situations like this, with all the confusing conflicting emotions, it's hard to tell whether feelings are real or pretended.

I left work immediately, canceling appointments, and went over to GB's to spend the afternoon talking. I didn't really know what to do, so I just listened and talked and said lots of stupid philosophical things and lots of even more stupid love-of-life sentimental things. He seemed depressed but not irrational—not that much different from usual. It was hard to believe that less than twenty-four hours before he was having his stomach pumped, on the verge of death. It was impossible to believe that he had really wanted to die—that he hadn't picked a place in the library where he was sure to be discovered in time. It had clearly been a grand cosmic gesture directed at Dennis Moyer. But even so, how could anyone as intelligent and fortunate as GB *do* such a thing? How could he even *risk* not being discovered in the library? The story didn't make sense to me; but I kept my doubts to myself, and we became a little closer because of the sleeping pill episode.

Somehow, that episode was over almost as fast as it had started. It wasn't talked about much; GB was not forced into analysis or a mental institution by the state, or whatever I somehow assumed they did to people who tried to kill themselves. Dennis, of course, had been very upset, but had determined not to lead GB on, under any circumstances. He felt that if he responded, he would keep the relationship alive and GB would keep torturing himself. If Dennis simply ceased to exist, GB would get over him. That's more or less the way it worked out. Dennis was the cross GB chose to bear, but GB managed to keep his romanticism in check and didn't eat any more sleeping pills.

Around Christmas, having been out of Yale now for two and a half years and out of the closet for six months, I slept with GB. Chris was on vacation from school, down in Alabama. There was no reason why GB and I shouldn't get together for dinner and a movie. But if Chris ever found out what we did afterward, he would be terribly upset.

To me, Chris's love was a mixed blessing. I liked having a handsome lover whom everyone else wanted. I liked having someone to call whenever I wanted to brag about my latest little coup at the office, whenever I wanted to describe this unbelievably hunky kid I saw pumping gas. But I am impatient by nature, and I was getting tired of driving Chris back and forth to Chase Hall through Harvard Square traffic or waiting for him to pick out the shirt he wanted to wear—hell, waiting for him to finish a sentence! That slow, easy drawl was beginning to get on my nerves. All that keeping-things-to-myself when I was a kid made me a private kind of individual. I couldn't take so much intimacy.

So when Golden Boy put his hand on my knee in his Maverick, with big snowflakes falling onto his windshield and onto the Christmas trees on the Common, I felt not the slightest compunction about making it with him. I didn't want to hurt Chris, but he would never know about it. If I could keep being gay a secret for a dozen years, surely I could keep quiet about a single night with GB. For his part, GB assured me he would never tell either—and how could he? It would wreck his friendship with Chris. So we were safe and Chris would not be hurt, and it didn't bother me to fool Chris, because really I was beginning to hope he would come back from Alabama with a crush on someone else.

As a matter of fact, that night Chris was in a gay bar in Atlanta. In the morning he was to interview Coke for a summer job, but that night he was out exploring the town. I know, because after the Coke interview he called to tell me what had happened at the bar. He had met this fellow, Rick, who was also just passing through Atlanta and doing some exploring. Nice-looking guy, Chris said, and I knew he was leading up to the confession that they had made it that night, and Chris just wanted to let me know that there was nothing to it and that he was looking forward to getting back to Boston . . . but no, that's not what had happened at all.

What happened was that Chris was telling Rick about Boston and about his lover John (me) who was a junior exec at IBM and—

"John what?" Rick apparently interrupted, suddenly showing real interest.

Chris told him my last name. "Holy shit! You're kidding! We used to work together in New York. You mean he was gay all that time?"

Meanwhile, of course, I was Holy shitting too as Chris told the story. You mean Rick Swidler, the kid who used to talk about the Italian women he had had. . . . You mean he was gay then?

Not only was he gay then, Chris told me, he had had a lover the whole time.

Anyhow, that was Rick, and the Coke interview went fine—how are things in Boston?

GB and I had a good time. Evidently, to my amazement, GB had wanted to do it with me for almost as long as I had wanted to do it with him, though I'm sure I hadn't loomed as large in his mind as he had in mine. The best-looking boy in the world and the best little boy in the world were beginning to open up to each other. He thought he was too tall, and he preferred dark hair to blond hair. He kind of wished he could be like me, with my job and all. Can you imagine? I told him how struck I had been when I first met him and how I had never dreamed we would become good friends. We agreed to go to the hospital to have a height transplant, bringing him down to six one and me up to five eleven.

The one thing he told me that I didn't like at all was that the whole suicide story had been nothing more than that—a story. He had just been feeling very depressed, he said, and had made up the whole thing. It was an attempted suicide without the attempt, the risk or the pain.

No one likes people who try to have their cake and eat it, too, and that's what this brand of attempted suicide seemed like to me. I felt duped. Used rather than needed. And it didn't do much for my impression of GB's stability. But then, he was only twenty-one, and he had never claimed to be the world's most stable class president. He was too romantic and imaginative to be entirely predictable and rational about everything—and perhaps that was the reason he was attracted by Dennis Moyer's pipe, his cool-head-edness, his reliability, and his established manner. Perhaps that's what he liked about my career at IBM. What could be more logical and rational and established than IBM, for crying out loud?

Anyway, I was past the idolizing stage with GB, and was now getting to know him on a realistic, good-with-the-bad, mortal basis.

Christmas came, and I went home to Brewster. I told Goliath that I wanted to talk with him about something and that we ought to go out back, out of earshot of the house, and build a snowman or something. Once Goliath had gone off to college, our relationship had improved immensely. I had been proud of my big brother at Yale, and he of his little brother, who would surely be admitted to Yale. We didn't see each other long enough to get on each other's nerves. So for the last ten years or so Goliath and I had been getting along famously, and I wanted to tell him what I had told all my other straight friends. I also wanted to know how he thought the Supreme Court would react if I told them.

Goliath was shocked. Coming from the same sheltered family I did, he knew as little about homosexuals as I would have if I hadn't happened to be one. Kind of like sickle-cell anemia—surely not the kind of disease that would strike anyone *he* knew. And here was his little brother, the one who had won all the varsity letters in high school which he, Goliath, had never been able to do, telling him that he was gay. Somewhere in the back of his mind he remembered a story his father had told him about what *his* father had done when he found out he had a homosexual history teacher.

Still, Goliath is no dummy, and blood runs thicker than

water, and I really didn't look or act any differently from the way I had always looked and acted, so perhaps I was going through a stage that a good shrink could hustle to a hasty conclusion.

No? Well, then, what could he say? He was terribly sorry for me and—

Goliath, you've got it all wrong. There is nothing for you to be sorry about, no need for sympathy. You didn't pay attention when I went through that long preface about this being good news, not bad news—that I had worked things out.

I proceeded to run through my sales pitch for homosexuality, which is something of an exercise in counting one's blessings:

After paying due respects to zero population growth and the ancient Greeks, Julius Caesar, and Tiberius, I went through my list of contemporaries—famous, productive, ostensibly happy people whom society admires without knowing they are gay. This may be a childish, "Johnny-did-it-too" kind of defense, perhaps even a subconscious exercise in "misery loves company," but it is gratifying all the same to see the mouths of wholesome Midwestern football fans gape when they hear the names of a couple of pro football players who are gay. Or politicians. Or actors. Or actresses. Or models. Or attorneys. Or Wall Street financiers. I obviously can't name names here, although it is curious that you can't be sued for calling a heterosexual a heterosexual or a black a black or a diabetic a diabetic. (As for the accuracy of my list, however, let me assure you that I have had the opportunity to do some "spot checking.")

Anyway, after adding a few fresh faces to Goliath's stereotyped crowd of hairdressers, interior designers, and sadistic concentration camp managers, I moved on to the more practical aspects of the way homosexuality would affect me.

I explained that without a family to support I could work half as hard or half as long to live just as well; or work just as hard and live twice as well. Or I could choose the kind of job I could otherwise not afford to take, but which offered some special nonmonetary rewards and satisfactions.

Of course, the price for this flexibility, independence, free time, and high living would be not having a wife and kids. I might have a lover, but I would certainly not have the joy of the model traditional family, like the one I grew up in.

But how many families are like the one I grew up in? What are the chances that a straight first marriage would end in a quick divorce, that a second would be to a girl I quickly tired of but tolerated for the sake of the children? It's no cinch being happy if you're straight either.

At this point in my pitch Goliath came in on cue and asked me about loneliness and about my later years. Who can argue with that? I learned aged twelve to twenty-three what it was like to be lonely, and I doubt I will ever be that lonely again—well, Christ, Goliath, don't you see that's one of the reasons I'm *telling* you all this and telling my straight friends? When I'm older, even if I haven't been able to find a guy to live my whole life with, which is not out of the question, I expect to have a number of truly close friends I know I can count on. Chris. Golden Boy. Hank. Brook. And others. Look, even if my straight friends got so wrapped up in their own families that they had no time or emotion to spare for me—which I don't think for a minute would be the case—I will have a circle of gay friends I can count on. They're in this, too, after all, and they will want to be able to count on me just as much as I will want to count on them. I may not be able to share the same toothbrush with Chris and spend every day with him, but (and now I'm jumping ahead of the story) he knows that there is *nothing* I wouldn't do for him and that he can count on me for the rest of my life. In return, I plan to count on him.

It won't be a family in the traditional sense, but I think I will have my own family of sorts. I won't have as much invested in any one person as I would with a traditional family, but I will have the benefits of diversification. I won't have kids to support me in my dotage—but it's easy enough to set yourself up for retirement. IBM and I have that well in hand.

Who will comfort me in the hospital bed when I am on the way out? Well, now you have asked a question to which I can't give a pat cheerful answer, and I admit it. Like you, I don't want to get old, and I very much don't want to die, and I will be one miserable old man lying in that bed if they haven't wised up to euthanasia by then. I have no answer to death, and let's change the subject.

Goliath and I went around and around for some time, but try as I might, I could not sell him on seeing a shrink to bring out whatever latent homosexuality he might have, hidden like a pearl within an oyster, in his head. But I did convince him over time that it would be equally foolish for me to go to a shrink to try to be "straightened out."

Before we drop this subject, I do think it is interesting to consider the question of Goliath's latent homosexuality. Rather, his apparent lack of any. How come? Not only did he come from the same family, he was the firstborn and as a result, one would assume, the more gingerly handled. By the time I came along my parents were probably less afraid of dropping me, less afraid that I would stick my tongue in the electric socket—and hell, if I did, at least they would still have Goliath. What's more, there *was* Goliath to terrorize me and to rough me up a little. Wouldn't this tend to have made my childhood *less* sheltered than his? Or was it that my parents tended to overprotect me from Goliath? And then there is the curious fact that in Goliath's crucial years, my father was off bombing Dresden, and Goliath was brought up with very little knowledge of his daddy. By the time I came along Daddy was back. Isn't it the kid *without* the daddy who is supposed to turn out gay?

Goliath and I went to the same schools, had many of the same teachers, went to the same camp—so what was the difference? Is homosexuality doled out at random? Was I just lucky? Or was it the fact that I was less hardy as a child—I did have a rough time with earaches when I was three or four—that led me to be more carefully protected? Or was it that my parents had decided to try out a different school of child psychology on me from the one they had used with Goliath, a psychology that somehow intensified my need for their love and attention, which thereby intensified my own desire to do only "good" things—and which made me feel guilty at the drop of a paint splotch? Or was I simply competing with Goliath for their attention in my most formative years, whereas Goliath had not had to compete in his own formative years—and was it this competition that made me determined to be the best little boy in the world?

Perhaps that last was it. More likely it was the sum of hundreds of different factors, all interrelated. I doubt that there is anything random about it. I know quite a few sets of gay brothers. I know one family of three gay brothers.

That suggests that people do not become gay at random. Homosexuality is an effect of causes, just like everything else in the world, even though the causes may be too legion or abstruse for us to fathom. And like all good effects, homosexuality is also a cause. A boy might develop homosexually *because* he was a meek child, while another might develop a meek personality once he realizes that he is a homosexual and therefore, according to society, inferior.

To me the case of Goliath and me suggests: First, if one or two of the sons turn out gay, that's neither good nor bad. It's the way it is. I am as happy as Goliath and as productive to society—and what else matters? Second, parents may as well give up on trying to keep their kids from growing up gay. A child's sexuality is too complicated to engineer.

Goliath and I went back into the house to check out the strings of Christmas tree lights we have been using for the past twenty-odd years. Tradition runs strong in our family. Every year we go to the same nursery to buy a tree a few days before Christmas. On the morning of Christmas Eve, Goliath and I try in vain to mount the tree on its stand, until finally our father is prevailed upon to level the tree's bottom through some miraculous gift he has (he is also one of those fathers who can put together Heathkit radios and get them to work) and set it up properly on the stand. We then bring the tree into the house, to the same spot in the living room each year, and our mother comes in to help us decide which side of the tree should be facing the wall and which facing out. Trees are deceptive that way. You keep turning them little by little, but the part that shows always seems to be less full of branches than it was a few seconds ago when it was facing the wall. Then we check the lights, just in time to run into town before the store closes if we need to replace some bulbs, and then, if the TV networks are willing, we settle down to *A Christmas Carol*, which is over just in time to rush out to the traditional Christmas Eve restaurant. When Goliath and I were young, that was often the only totally peaceful, harmonious meal of the year. Then we drive back home, always by nine-thirty, no fighting in the car, and my mother always says that we have never gotten home so late before and that she doesn't see how we can possibly get everything done before midnight. I needn't explain the importance of getting everything done before midnight, need I? So she starts decorating the dining-room table with little men in sleighs while Goliath and I start wiring up the tree. Dad fiddles with the FM tuner he constructed long ago, trying to find the perfect station for an evening like this. Eventually, he sits down in his chair, feet stretched comfortably over the ottoman that was once the scene of my paint-splotches-on-the-lawn spanking, and like Walter Cronkite in the command post, oversees the preparation of Apollo 14, or, in this case, the tree. When the electrical work is done, Mom appears to express her amazement at the way we have managed to arrange the lights so beautifully and to help with the hundreds of snowballs and glittering pine cones and delicate tinsel balls that we have come to know so well. Inevitably, Goliath drops an ornament whose delicate spire breaks off—but the feeling is too good on this night for any recrimination. Dad moves from his command post to take the ornament down to the basement for some glue and hidden supports, and half an hour later, back on the tree it goes. My mother is sure this is the best-looking tree we have ever done. But it is now nearly eleven, for crying out loud, and we still have to wrap the presents and write the poems!

The poems, excepting the occasional fluke, are terrible. The meter is off, the puns are awful, but they will be received with delight in the morning when it is finally time to come downstairs and open the presents.

I find myself tempted to describe our Christmas Eve ritual in the past tense, because it is filed in my childhood memories. Yet there is really no reason for that, because next Christmas Eve will be exactly as I have described past ones. If anyone should appreciate the joys of a nearly perfect family, it is me. I know only a handful of friends whose parents have had such storybook marriages and whose families have been so close. Well, I suppose we are the best little family in the world. Yet I doubt that I will envy Hank's beautiful family, when he has one, any more than he will envy my independent and fulfilling life-style.

I left Brewster to go back to work. Chris had said he would be coming back in time for New Year's.

For Christmas I had sent him two of my favorite albums: Peter, Paul and Mary's *Album 700*, which I had first heard with Hank at Yale, and Tom Rush's *Circle Game*, with Brook. Back in Boston I found that Chris had sent me *The Guinness Book of World Records*—perhaps so the best little boy in the world would know what his competition was. Did you know, for example, that "The duration record for lying on a bed of nails (needle-sharp 6-inch 2 inches apart) is 25 hours 9 minutes"?

One of my project workers at the office, with whom I had become quite close, gave me a Playboy Club Key for Christmas. I couldn't resist taking him there for dinner to tell him about his boss's sexual preferences. I had passed the stage of "Sit down, Sam, there's something I want to tell you." That was too melodramatic and serious and self-important. I would simply answer questions honestly if they happened to come up. So, when my Playboy friend asked me who I was sleeping with these days, I said, "Chris." Then I answered the questions that followed. I liked this approach because it put being gay in the proper light: not something dreadful to be ashamed of and whispered about; just something to be good-naturedly discussed.

CHAPTER 13

I had developed ugly, but uncontrollable, reflexes to inconsequential things Chris did. He had a way of clearing his throat that was like the toast-scraping cliché. It annoyed me. Of course, the annoyance was only a manifestation of some greater annoyance with our relationship. Perhaps what annoyed me most was that the BLBITW had the capacity to be so selfish, so impatient, so ugly.

I went to the airport to pick up Chris, hoping our two-week Christmas separation would somehow have given me the breather I needed. I wanted to be able to enjoy his needing me, not resent it. I wanted to want to be with him.

Though two weeks had passed, I found myself feeling even more hyper than usual as I sat waiting for his delayed flight. I just don't have time for this! I have important work at the office, two proposals that will knock their eyes out if I ever get time to finish writing them. I haven't even had time to fill out my expense voucher for last month, and here I am on a plastic chair in the Eastern Airlines terminal accomplishing zilch and waiting for god-damned Christopher and the god-damned way he has of clearing his god-damned throat. What am I *doing* here? You're slowing me down, Chris. You're holding me back.

Was it Chris, or would any mortal affect me the same way? Did this experience mean that I would never be able to have more than a few weeks' fling with anyone? That question was the crux of it, and it was not fun to think about.

The next four months went well enough, more or less on my terms. We talked on the phone every day but only got together a couple of times a week and went out on our own a lot. As far as I was concerned, Chris was a good friend. As far as he was concerned, I was his lover. We blamed the infrequency with which we got together on our respective work loads: his three business school cases a night, my projects at IBM. That was less painful than trying to explain it in terms of what was really happening.

I was happy. I had the advantages of the relationship without the claustrophobia. I made friends with a lot of other people. I thought we would just drift apart. Surely by June, when Chris went down South for his summer job, things would just naturally come to an end. I knew Chris too well to think he could spend a whole summer without finding lots of other people to replace me. When he returned in the fall, we would be good friends—I did want that—but we would be free of each other.

In fact, the end came even before the summer, late in April. But first I should introduce some of the people I met in the months before that disastrous April.

Some of them, like Rick Swidler from IBM, were faces from the past. I ran into two of my old high school classmates, both of whom had apparently been active even back then. One described the affair he had had with our music teacher, aged fourteen and thirty-two respectively. The other claimed to have been "experimenting" with some of the stars of the class, many of the ones I had been dying to befriend, though not with Brian.

Where *was* Brian? Neither of my two fellow alumni knew. The last I knew of Brian was that he had been expelled two days before our graduation. He had been sitting in the back of a large lecture room. One of our more conservative teachers, who used to sprinkle his patriotic lectures with long pauses, placed at random to emphasize his failing mind, was giving one of the final sermons of the year in our American history class. People were fidgeting and rustling and snapping and clicking and whispering, bored to tears, thinking of the GTO's they had been promised for graduation, but our mentor pressed on. He was saying that teachers should be investigated by the FBI before they were allowed near the pliable young minds of our great nation. "Such a system would"—pause—"be worth the inconvenience it"—pause—"would cause and the"—pause—"indignation it would no doubt arouse among some of"—pause—"the fanatics we have teaching"—pause—"today. But it would eliminate unsavory"—pause—"and subversive people like—"

"You!" Brian stage-whispered to his friends in the back of the room. Unfortunately, at that moment there was a lull in the shuffling and rustling, and Brian was expelled two days before graduation. You won't believe this next part, but no matter: His father sent him off to a school for rich dumb kids in need of high school diplomas—in Wyoming. I have heard nothing of him since.

I was in Sporters one night and saw a former acquaintance from Yale walk in with a girl. I thought they might have walked in by mistake, or to use the phone, or that they both might have been gay. When they didn't go running back out, but ordered drinks, I walked over to Bill and said hi. He was wearing jeans and a blue Chemise Lacoste shirt, just like the one I had on. He looked a little embarrassed and explained that he and his girl had been out drinking and thought they would come in here to see what a queer bar was like. This is what it's like, I told him, describing some of the other kinds of bars and ordering a drink myself. He was with one of the Boston banks, he said; I was at IBM. I could see he couldn't quite believe he was having a conversation like this with me in a gay bar—why wasn't I begging him not to tell anyone he saw me and all that?—and he was embarrassed that it might look as though he thought of all this as a freak show he had come to watch. "We didn't come in to sneer, just out of curiosity," he reassured me several times, sounding very much the budding Boston Brahmin, even if slurring some of his words. His date was silent. Bill didn't want to offend me, so he kept saying how surprised he was that this was what the bar was like, how impressed he was. What did he mean, I wanted to know. "Well, everyone is so well *behaved*," he said. He kept repeating that.

"We must have lunch sometime," Bill said in parting, but he never called me, and I spared him. What would his fellow bankers think if he were having lunch with me right in the middle of Locke-Ober's and all of a sudden I forgot myself and did something perverted?

Another time in Sporters—I spent a lot of time in Sporters those first two years—I met Hank's Harvard Law School roommate, Parker Martinson III. (Later Hank moved off-campus with a really super girl, but his first year he shared a room with Parker Martinson III.) Parker, Hank, and I had been friends back at Yale.

Parker is an emotional, excitable type. You'd say, "Parker! Look at that giant carrot behind your left ear!" and invariably he would turn to look. When he turned back to find his butterscotch pudding gone, he would make a big thing about it: "Jeez, why do you always *pick* on me?" If he came into the room wearing an expensive new sport coat and said, "Don't I look great?" and you said, obviously fooling, that it looked just like the one they buried Charlemagne in, he would take great offense and start whining. Parker wanted attention; he wanted to have his feelings hurt. And now here he was in Sporters.

"Parker!" I said loudly, slapping him on the shoulder from behind, feeling sure I would evoke one of his more classic reactions. It's not often you meet someone you know from "the real world" in the bar.

"Oh, my God!" Parker sort of yelped, wide-eyed. He was pale. "John, you've got to *promise* me you will never tell anyone about this. Promise me."

"Okay. I promise. But *tell* me, Parker—this is great!—how long have you been doing this? Tell me everything." I was beaming again, sure that Parker would quickly overcome his initial fright and start to beam, too. Well, it's like being alone in Tokyo and running across an old friend. We could speak the same language. Super.

"First promise me."

"I promise! Tell me!"

Apparently, Parker had been going to gay bars, and other places, for *four years* now—"Parker! You're a pro! If only *I* had been out at Yale!"—and he had *never* met anyone from the real world before. He had dreaded this moment for four years. All his work dating girls and making up alibis, shattered.

"Promise me you will never tell Hank!"

"Tell Hank what?" I grinned.

"Come on, John, you know what!" he said in his why-were-we-always-picking-on-him tone of voice.

"What? That you're gay? He wouldn't care. I told him about me and—"

"You what!" Parker moved forward a little, and his hands went out to the sides, the way you would move if you were opening a double door, only he forgot there was a drink in his right hand, and half of it sloshed out of the glass, narrowly missing a piano-tuner friend of mine.

"Relax, Parker! I promise I won't tell Hank about *you*, but when I told him about me, it just made us closer."

"Promise me you will never tell a soul you met me here!" Well, I had no intention of exposing or blackmailing Parker Martinson, but I was getting just a trifle miffed that he had so little faith in my discretion. I mean, I had already promised him three times now, and he was still asking me to promise him. I decided to show him how ridiculous he was beginning to sound, by being sarcastic:

"No, Parker, I am going over to that pay phone there—oh! look at that knock-out by the phone! Maybe I can kill two birds with one phone"—I was on my third beer, so excuse me—"and I'm going to call your mother. Is there more than one Martinson in the Baltimore phone directory? Oh, that doesn't matter, I forgot. If you're the third, then your father's name must be Parker, too."

Parker was aghast and at least pretended that he took me seriously. He kept imploring me not to call. I kept asking him to lend me a dime.

But this was too ridiculous. How could anyone as bright as Parker, who had been out for four years, for crying out loud, not pick up on my sarcasm and just shut up? How could he be so paranoid?

"Parker. *Shut up!* In the first place, I haven't the slightest reason to tell anyone I met you in here, and I've promised three times that I won't. In the second place, you should be delighted you met me. Stop being so paranoid and start being delighted." I sounded very authoritative. Parker calmed down.

Parker had been dealing with his homosexuality—rather, his bisexuality, as he was quick to define it—differently from me. Not only had he never told any of his straight friends he was gay, but he also went by a phony name in the bar and never brought anyone home to his place or gave out his phone number. He almost never saw anyone twice. He would just sit at home, his horniness for a guy building up and hating himself for that, and finally he would give in and go out hunting. After he had had sex with a guy, generally under the raunchiest, most impersonal conditions, he would invariably resolve to go straight from that moment on. To paraphrase the stale cigarette-quitting joke: He had gone straight a hundred times in the last four years.

I thought Parker should have been delighted to see me because after four years he had finally found someone to talk to. I knew what it was like to go for years without having anyone to talk with about Topic No. 1, and I assumed he was bursting.

I was right. Parker and I have talked almost every day over the last year and a half since I met him in the bar. I guess I'm his closest friend. Our friendship is special for me, too. My close straight friends and my close gay friends tend to be handsome. Parker is not. My customary rationalization for having mostly attractive friends is: There are more good people around than you'll ever have time to get to know, anyway, so you may as well choose the ones who are attractive. But a world in which looks are so important is a pretty lousy, terribly inequitable world. I find myself a little more palatable for my friendship with Parker.

So Parker Martinson was gay. What do you know? I *told* you Hank was attractive. Not that Parker had any more idea of making it with Hank than I had. I had to smile when I reflected that not only had two of Hank's several roommates over the years been gay without his knowing it (he still doesn't know about Parker) but so was his boss at the part-time job he held down. Hank was surrounded by us and didn't know it.

I don't mention this to make you feel uncomfortable, as though there were this creepy, insidious plot to surround good-looking all-American boys with unwholesome perverts who plan to corrupt the world when the time is right. This coincidence is worth mentioning simply for what it says about a lot of gay people: They are just like everybody else; you wouldn't know they were gay unless they told you. (Some, I'm told, are even very well behaved.)

To readers who resent my spelling out such an obvious and trite message, I can only plead the Sophistication Gap. On one side of the gap you have gay people and some straight people, mainly Spiro's effete snobs, I think, who know all about homosexuality and couldn't care less. Of course, they would rather their *own* sons didn't grow up gay, because that strikes some sensitive intimate chords, but they enjoy the company of their gay friends. On this side of the gap myself, I keep having to remind myself of the other side—of all the people George McGovern had in mind when he asked the Democratic Convention not to commit political suicide by endorsing "The Right to Be Different." On this other side of the gap are Jon Martin's friend's parents, who disowned their son the Yale graduate because he was gay. Hell, my Playboy-Club-Key project-worker friend went to Arizona State and to Stanford B-School and reads the *New York Times* every day, but when I mentioned to him recently that a guy we had just passed on the street was "in drag," he said: "What's 'drag'?" (It's a guy dressing up like a girl—but can there really be people who don't know that?)

One rainy Saturday afternoon I went to see the double bill at the Harvard Square Cinema. I like going to movies alone, curling up in a nearsighted row with no one around me and becoming totally absorbed in the picture. I found myself standing in line next to a boy in a Harvard crew sweat shirt and track shoes, whose name was probably something like Doug Decathlon. My knees went a trifle wobbly.

There was nobody with him, and I wanted to think of something to say to make conversation. Yet anything I said to this guy would be motivated by my attraction to him, and, even if he didn't, *I* would know it was a despicable "approach." He turned to me, smiled, and said, "Hi. Howya doin'?"

I was fine, and I wondered whether he really rowed for

the Harvard crew, as his sweat shirt suggested, because a friend of mine had been on the crew at Yale. (Such an astounding coincidence.) Pete (it was Pete, not Doug) did row for Harvard and had narrowly missed going to the Olympics.

The first sentence you hear someone say often tells you 90 percent of all you will ever know about that person. How many years of school did he sit through, where is he from, where on the scale from formal to flipped-out, where on the scale from self-confident to insecure, where on the scale from genuine to affected. Sometimes at Sporters you go up to someone of apparent cowboy potential and the first words out of his mouth say: "I'm from Queents, New Yawuk, and my life'ss ambition iss to go to Porto Rico and find some gorgeouss number to fuck me." In contrast, Pete sounded as all-American as you please.

As he was buying his ticket, my palms began to sweat. I could think of absolutely no way to ask another guy to sit next to me in a movie without sounding queer. He waited for me to buy my ticket and asked me where I liked to sit. "Ya-ha-ha," I gurgled.

The first movie was *Women in Love*, which all my friends had told me to see and all the critics loved. I am too impatient and businesslike to enjoy a movie like that. The photography was beautiful, but nothing *happened*. I was bored with *Women in Love*. Even the famous nude wrestling scene left me cold.

While we were waiting for the next movie to start, a good one, I thought it would be safe to talk with him about homosexuality. Not mine, needless to say; the homosexuality in *Women in Love*. Pete seemed to know a good bit about the subject, but not enough to incriminate himself.

The next movie was *The Great Escape*, starring Steve McQueen in lots of implausible action. I gobbled it up, middle-brow all the way, and then tried to get Pete back to our interrupted discussion as we were filing out. I said it was amazing how many people were gay—I had even heard a rumor that Steve McQueen was gay. (I hadn't, but Pete couldn't know that, and it fit the conversation because we had just spent two hours watching him being masculine.) Pete, who I was beginning wishfully to think just might be about where I had been when I was twenty, said he hadn't heard that rumor and hoped it wasn't true—it would ruin his image of Steve McQueen, he said.

As we were leaving the theater, the sun down by now and faint claps of distant thunder in my stomach, I decided to invite him back for dinner. Why not? Why should I feel guilty about asking him over, so long as I planned to do nothing improper? But before I could ask him, *he asked me.*

What's going on? He is thinking all the things I'm thinking, I think, but he isn't really, is he? Or is he?

We had dinner at his off-campus apartment. A little white wine, talk about Harvard and Yale, talk about the stadiums he had to run, up and down those steps twenty times, to keep in shape; talk about WBCN and the Firesign Theatre, about the draft, about how he was coming with his thesis. "Well, look, thanks a lot," I said. "I hope you'll come over to my place for dinner sometime." (Or, as the young man in the American Museum of Natural History once put it, "Now let me show you what interests me.")

He called a couple of nights later to see whether I wanted to hear Pete McCloskey talk about the war, and I said sure, why didn't he come over first since we had a couple of hours before it started? When he came over, after a little preliminary talk, I told him I was gay. He perked up. "I'm glad you told me that," he said, because he was sometimes attracted to guys. Well, he was attracted to me. But whenever he had tried to talk about the general subject with any of his friends, they put him down and wouldn't talk about it.

Well, I would talk about it until I got cramps in my jaw if he wanted. Attracted to *me*! Hot dog. Of course he had a steady girlfriend and would surely marry and have kids, but he had always thought it was a shame that guys couldn't express what they felt for other guys.

We missed the McCloskey talk and rambled on for hours about our respective hangups and inclinations and backgrounds and life-styles. I was a very good boy. I liked Pete too much, wanted him to like me too much, to ruin it with any horny ideas. If it was going to happen, it would happen, but I wanted our friendship to be more than just a means to get him into bed. Or was I such a gentleman because I sensed the only way to make it with him was to pretend I didn't care about that, only about our friendship? How much of "love," particularly early in a relationship, is based on sex? How much on friendship? Of friendship between two guys who are eight or nine on my scale? Of charisma? More than the romantic in us would care to admit, I think.

It happened.

Once it did, my burning, romantic desire to be Pete's close friend abated a good bit.

I'm surprised I went home with Ernie. He lived at Radcliffe, which was strange enough. Who would ever have thought *I* would be screwing around at Radcliffe? Well, who would ever have thought Harvard guys would be living there, and Radcliffe girls living in Harvard dorms? But stranger still, Ernie is black. Well chocolate. Growing up in New York made me a guilty liberal, anxious to see blacks get their fair share—and it made me nervous. I see a black guy coming toward me late at night, I get nervous. I see four black guys coming toward me, I get very nervous. This despite the fact that throughout my entire sheltered existence my only "mugging," and a nonviolent one at that, occurred when I was five, with Goliath in the park—and the mugger was white and about ten years old.

Objectively, I see many handsome black guys. Subjectively, they register low on my preppie dial, my cowboy dial, my wish-I-could-be-like-him dial. I don't wish I were black. Nor am I into the black-master-white-slave trip some people are. Or even the white-master-black-slave trip. (I do have one friend, married with kids, whose sole homosexual experience was in college, where he had this craving to be debased at the feet of a big black classmate. He felt so *guilty* being a rich young WASP, or at least that had something to do with it.)

Anyway, Ernie is such a handsome guy I always think of him as a model for one of those four-color Jamaican rum ads in *Playboy* or *Esquire*. He's just under six feet tall, or just over if you don't press down the Afro when you measure, and he is the picture of health and proper proportion. His father is a doctor in California, where Ernie was the token black in his suburban high school class. The prep school tradition isn't as big on the West Coast as the Andover-Exeter tradition is back East, but the kind of school he went to was a close equivalent. I guess it might be likened to

Scarsdale High. He was a shoo-in to Harvard, the kind of applicant who brings a moment of tranquillity and joy to the consciences on the besieged admissions committee: "No question, boys: We'd want this man for the class of '77 if he were white, green or purple."

I have an idea I know why Ernie was gay. Rather similar, really, to the situation that I think made me gay. There he was, black, in the library doing his homework when all his "brothers" were out shooting hoops. He was learning trigonometry while they were learning to kick ass in the street. Not that he knew any of his "brothers" personally—his parents didn't want him mixing with hooligan elements—but *everyone* knows that the brothers are tough street fighters and that they do naughty things. Well, Ernie became as frightened as I did when he saw four blacks walking toward him. His special fear was that he knew he wasn't really a man. He wasn't a black, and he wasn't a white. He was a phony.

One way to compensate, of course, was for Ernie to work out with weights and go out for sports; he didn't *look* weaker than his brothers, by any means. But inside, he felt less tough. He felt different. He wished he could be Leroy Stud.

Straight blacks and gay whites have much in common. Harlem and Roxbury are analogous to Greenwich Village and Beacon Hill. The black subculture has its jive, the gay subculture its camping and dishing. Some blacks overcompensate with Cadillacs; some gays overcompensate with motorcycles. Blacks are consciously trying to promote black pride, gays, gay pride. Most of society, perhaps despite itself, just doesn't feel comfortable with either group. They're okay if they stay in their place, but not running the Department of Defense, say, or dating my son. Even "liberals" feel uncomfortable just talking with blacks or gays: having to think carefully about everything they say, so as not to offend inadvertently, but not so carefully as to be obvious, which is offensive in itself. And there are those blacks and gays with chips on their shoulders who *want* to take offense and who can find reason to in almost anything.

Just as blacks in a predominantly white society are inordinately conscious of their color, gays in a predominantly straight society are inordinately conscious of their sexuality. Constant awareness of a socially undesirable trait can be debilitating, alienating, embittering. It can make you paranoid or just plain bitchy. In any case, it will have a profound effect. Not the skin color itself—that will determine only the degree to which you reflect light and can hide in dark corners. It is the "wrongness" of the color that will get you. Not the sexual orientation itself—that will determine only whom you want to sleep with. It is the wrongness of the orientation that will get you. In both cases, it is the prejudice, not the condition, that does the harm. It may be, as some would have it, that blacks are inherently inferior to whites or that homosexuals are all, by definition, sick. So what? Even if either condition truly is inherently undesirable, no manner of social pressure will turn blacks into whites or gays into straights. Social pressure will only exaggerate the handicap. It is still the prejudice, more than the condition, that does the harm.

Two differences between gays and blacks are worth noting, too. Some people may not like blacks, but they can hardly argue that blackness is immoral, that blacks should be painted white. By contrast, many still feel that homosexuality is "bad," that homosexuals should be treated to make them heterosexuals. And, if you are black, everyone knows it. It's just a physical property, though it has its effect on the mind as the mind develops. But if you are gay, it can be (must be) hidden. It is *all* in your mind. Tangible manifestations may follow, as in manner of dress or speech—but conceivably there could be five or ten or twenty million men and women walking around this country whom everybody assumes are straight, but who are actually gay.

Given the social and career costs of being gay, most of those who are not obvious are not going to wave any flags. A white newsman or politician can join the fight for racial equality without any fear that people will suspect he is black. Can a straight male do the same for the gay cause?

I met Charlie on the second floor of the Doubleday Bookstore where they filmed those scenes in *The Owl and the Pussycat.* I was in New York on business. My friend Freddie (of the oral virus) had met Charlie some time back in the Boston Public Library and thought he was a terrific guy I should meet. So I called Charlie, who said something about any friend of Freddie's being a friend of his, and why didn't we meet up there by the New Titles rack?

Charlie is refreshingly conservative. Besides his natural, rugged appearance (no hair dryers and Guccis for him, even if he does live in New York), he never goes to bars, never blows dope, never talks about how he is dying to go to bed with so-and-so. He is not promiscuous. Instead, his energies go into a hundred enterprises, from painting the hallway of his building to cutting some ivy from City Hall for his friends (it grows back), to going for a bike ride, to baking banana bread. He runs on just a few hours' sleep, never complains about anything, even about New York. He loves

New York. He is always busy and happy. I run on like this because I stand amused and awed by his marvelous good spirits. He is what I think they call "well adjusted."

Freddie was right, we did hit it off well. Charlie was so different from most of the people I met who would have taken me to the bars, or maybe a movie, and then back to their place to have sex. Charlie had me drive around the city and showed me where all the notable buildings were with little stories about their architecture and all—boring, but different—and then at one in the morning he said, "You know what we should do now? You may not want to, but I hope so." Well, I knew what he had in mind, and I wanted to. "We should drive to the tip of Manhattan and take the Staten Island Ferry for a nickel." *What?*

That was typically Charlie. He is gay with straight, old-fashioned ideas. It was only later that I realized one reason for Charlie's self-control was that he had a lover, an executive at Bristol Myers with whom he shared a townhouse. Still, sex seems less on Charlie's mind than on most, and that is appealing.

"Imagine my surprise," therefore, when one evening visiting Charlie, after dinner and a bottle of wine, he said he wanted to show me something he had only shown a few of his closest friends. I thought maybe he was going to drop his pants or something, which never does as much for me as it's supposed to—but then he reached behind a cabinet and pulled out a manilla envelope. Inside was a magazine of gay pornography.

Really, Charles, you are too much. I mean, prudishness is one thing, but to be secretive about a silly porno mag. I mean *every*body has them or has seen them. I was thinking this as I looked through the thirty-two pages of color photographs of two nude males doing various things—I prefer pictures with pants, like in *Sports Illustrated* or the back of *Esquire*, but I look through the hard-core stuff when it is offered—and even Charlie shouldn't make such a big deal out of a magazine like that.

"One of my odd jobs," he said. "I'd rather you didn't mention it to people, but I thought you'd get a—"

"*Wait a minute!* Is that *you*?"

He grinned half-sheepishly, half-proudly as I looked back and forth between him and the better-looking of the two guys doing all those disgusting things in full unairbrushed color.

"How much did they pay you for that?" I had to ask.

"A hundred bucks."

I could describe lots of other people I met that first gay winter in Boston, but to do so would be stalling. It's just that it is difficult to write about breaking up with Chris that April; when I think about it, I still wince.

That month Chris met Hunter, a divinity student who was in the throes of breaking up with his lover of the last four years, a naval ensign stationed in Newport, Rhode Island. I first heard about Hunter from Golden Boy, who described him as the kind of guy Chris might easily get hung up on if he were not already hung up on me. Fine. By now Chris and I were talking every day, but getting together for dinner only once or twice a week and not always staying overnight. No doubt, as he saw more of Hunter, he would see less of me, and gradually, painlessly, he would have a new lover, and I would still be his good friend.

Instead, Golden Boy decided to speed things up. He thought I was being unfair stringing Chris along the way I was and not simply cutting off our relationship so he would feel free to get deeply involved with Hunter.

I went down to the bar one evening and saw Chris looking darkly at his bottle of beer. Hi! He was cool to me. What's wrong? "Maybe there's been a lot wrong for a long time that I didn't know about." What do you mean? I had a feeling I knew what he meant, but it was inconceivable that Golden Boy could have told him. "If you don't know what I mean, maybe we should just forget it." I was beginning to feel knots inside. "We'll still talk every day, won't we?" Tears had come to my eyes. "Maybe we'd better not." I looked into his eyes and put my fists to my own eyes to keep anyone from seeing the tears as I ran out to my car.

I know this won't do much for the Joe College image I want you to have of me, but it's what happened. Usually I was in good control of myself. But I suddenly felt such an overwhelming sadness for having hurt Chris and at the thought that I might lose his love. Not his body, his love.

I called Golden Boy and asked him why he had done it, why he had told Chris. He said he had hated seeing Chris torn between Hunter and me when I didn't really love him. He was sorry, but he thought it was for the best.

What a crazy thing to do! It would have to ruin the friendship he had with Chris, mine with Chris, mine with Golden Boy.

The next few weeks were painful for all of us, as painful as any I've ever experienced. All the cold analysis in the world, with which I could ordinarily manipulate my emotions, wouldn't make the unhappiness go away. I felt dreadful that I had hurt Chris so badly. I felt awfully lonely without talking with him every day. I had to make up for it somehow, I had to make him understand what it was about me that made me the way I was, I had to get him to forgive me, and we had to stay best friends.

I knew I was not ready, if I ever would be, for a full-time kind of relationship. Sometimes the romantic in me tried to fool me into thinking I could handle it—but I knew the moment I had managed to persuade Chris to lower his defenses again and need me, I would again want to be free.

I spent hours writing to Chris, talking with Chris, trying to make him see why I couldn't be his lover but had to be his best friend. Whether or not it fit the textbook definition of why, how, and when to love someone, I loved Chris now. Would he forgive me? Could we count on each other for good?

Chris said he couldn't just turn off his love for me. He said he had built up defenses to ward off the hurt, and he agreed that we would never be full-time exclusive partners in life. But he said he would always love me.

Good things don't come easily. I think the intense pain the three of us felt soldered a bond that really will last a long, long time.

More than a year has passed since that April, and Chris and I have talked or seen each other almost every day. Hunter, while he was around, understood. Hunter was number one, of course, but there could be other people in Chris's life, like me and Golden Boy. Golden Boy, too, was forgiven. The crisis was over, and now I loved Chris.

Sex has nothing to do with this love; it may be only the fear of loneliness. What I think this love is, is a fabric of shared experiences and feelings, woven only with great effort over time. That's why I think it will only grow stronger.

There is no "right guy" or "right girl" out there waiting to be discovered. There is only the hard work of building and investing in a relationship—and I have invested in Chris.

CHAPTER 14

More than a year has passed since Chris and Golden Boy and I had our minor catastrophe, and I am about to move down to Washington. One of the "two proposals that would knock their eyes out" at IBM, which I alluded to earlier, did. I got a fat raise and was asked to move to Washington to supervise fulfillment of the accepted proposal. First, though, I was to take the vacation time I had accumulated, which I've spent writing this.

This past year has been a good one, and a little less frantic than the one before. I have lost much of my compulsion to make up for lost time: I've caught up with myself. Having packed several years' growing up into just a couple, all I have to do now is grow up a year at a time, which should, relatively speaking, be a snap.

Like anyone, I think a lot about what my life will be like in the future. How can I best take advantage of being gay and minimize the disadvantages? I've met a variety of people whose life-styles have helped me see some of the alternatives open to me for "later life."

I met Bob Knight the first summer I came out. Peter-who-does-the-thing-with-the-ice and I were walking along the river toward one of the Boston Pops outdoor concerts, when we ran into Rob-the-mute-math-whiz and this very handsome guy, Bob Knight. He had his shirt off, draped over his back with just the sleeves hanging down the front.

I tried to be cool about it. I sensed that looking at Bob while talking with Rob or Peter was no way to score points with anyone, but I couldn't help myself. I came on too strong. I don't remember all the things I said to Bob, but I remember asking for his phone number and calling him several times, only to hear that he was busy. Some weeks later I asked Peter what I had done wrong. He told me that if the Germans had employed my subtle approach in World War I, they could have pushed through the Maginot Line in a week and a half.

A year later, which is to say a year ago, I met Bob at a party. He was dressed differently, verging on "piss elegant," and he sounded more affected than he had the summer before. I could swear he had lost some of his "masculinity." Why was he letting it slip away? Surely he noticed the difference in himself, no?

Three months ago someone walked into Sporters who was beautiful in a way too "graceful" to interest me—until I realized that it was *Bob* wrapped up in that silk ascot, with something very like a handbag slung over his shoulder. It was the same body, softened somewhat and carried differently. It was the same face, only the expression was somehow less natural, facial muscles "just so." And the voice—"My *dear*, was Miss Knight affected!"

Why do so many people follow this progression? Is it really that we all wish we were women and that we simply follow the logical path as fast as we can lower our inhibitions? Does the logical path lead to gowns, lipstick, and Scandinavian surgery?

For some it seems to. Yet I think much of the apparent femininity in the gay world is attributable to subcultural style rather than to an inner desire to be feminine. For example:

When I first came out, I noticed, disapprovingly, that most gays call each other by their formal first names. In a straight football huddle you would hear, "All right, Joe, you go long; McMicking, you go wide; Albie, you . . ."—not "Joseph, you go long; Martin, you go wide; Albert, you . . ." So when I made friends with a guy introduced as Raymond, I called him Ray. Everyone else called him Raymond, and at least at first, I would wince imperceptibly when they did, and maybe feel a bit superior. But gradually, over many months of hearing him called nothing but Raymond, it began to sound more and more like his name. Ray sounded wrong. Somewhere along the line I started calling him Raymond. Was that a loss of masculinity? Was it caused by an inner desire to be a woman? Or isn't it natural to conform to the styles around you unless you make a conscious effort not to? In fact, because I do worry about silly things like this, I have reverted to calling him Ray. But if I worked in a largely gay environment, rather than at IBM, and if I weren't so hung up on my Brooks Brothers self-image, mightn't I call people by their formal first names? Mightn't I laugh when friends camped and in turn camp to make them laugh? Would I be doing it because deep down I wish I were a woman? Would my doing it make me somehow inferior?

I doubt that I will go the way of Bob Knight as I get older. Not because I think there is anything "wrong" with carrying a pocketbook—or a chain, for that matter. Just wrong for me, for the image I want of myself.

My lawyer is forty-three. He grew up in New Jersey, the only child of a powerful mother. He went to the University of Wisconsin, to U.Va. Law School, to Korea, and to the law firm that represents IBM. I say "my lawyer," though I have never had reason to engage him. I just worked with him occasionally in the course of my first years at IBM in New York. We became friendly enough that if anyone had ever decided to sue me for playing my stereo too loud and demanded the name of "my lawyer," I would have felt comfortable giving him the name of this man, Something Something, Esq., hereinafter referred to as Esquire.

Esquire carries a Samsonite attaché, or did until recently; lives on the twenty-third floor of a swank East Side apartment building (the kind without elevator men, but with TV cameras in the elevators to keep you from raping fellow tenants); wears a wedding band, though he is separated from his wife; and is remarkably dapper and trim for someone his age.

About a year and a half ago I was back down in New York on business, and I called Esquire to see if he wanted to have dinner. With his wife gone he had a lot of evenings free and had told me to call him for lunch or dinner any time I was in the city. I should come up to his place, and we would go from there, he said.

His $500-a-month (I'm guessing) one-bedroom apartment sent gay bleeps into my radar, bleeps that would probably not show up on a straight screen, like the tube of K-Y in the medicine chest or the Barbra Streisand albums among his record collection. I wondered: Could Esquire be gay? I remembered the time we had played handball on his membership at the New York Athletic Club (no blacks and only twelve Jews allowed, but some faggots and lots of closet cases) and what remarkably good shape he was in. I wondered why he had separated from his wife and why they had had no children.

At the restaurant, I thought I noticed him noticing the same busboy I was noticing as my herring and his vichyssoise were delivered. What a pleasant coincidence, I thought, as I made up my mind to try to spill a spoonful of vichyssoise into his well-tailored lap. "Esquire," I said, "I think you should be cognizant of the kinds of matters you might have to defend me against. So I think"—the timing was important here so I paused long enough in the count down for him to dip his spoon into the soup—"I should tell you"—head was bending a little and spoon emerging with its payload—"that I am"—eyes beginning to widen as mission control prepared for docking of the silver soup shuttle—"gay." *Contact!*

Damn. I could see the spoon rattle around a little as it began to enter his mouth, but surface tension, which if I remember my high school chemistry right increases with viscosity, and so is stronger in vichyssoise than in water, kept any from spilling.

"You are?" he asked, upon swallowing. He sounded disapproving.

"I am." Maybe I was wrong about Esquire, though as far as I was concerned, he could know in any case.

"Why are you telling *me*?"

"Well, I thought as my lawyer you should know. That's all. No big thing, just file it away somewhere in your head so when I get busted for dancing with a plainclothesman I won't have to waste my one-phone-call dime giving you the background."

He must have decided I wasn't trying to trap him. "All right then," he said, "would you like to go to a party with me after dinner?" He still wasn't smiling, and I could tell he was worried and upset that I had apparently assumed he was gay. What was wrong with his cover? Could others tell? Was it too much aftershave, or what?

"A party? What do you mean?" I asked, thinking it would be only considerate to let him make his revelation to me. He told me he was gay, also, but wondered whether I could tell. I said that I am always suspicious of guys his age who were so good-looking and living alone—but that's not why I had told him I was gay. A party? Sure, let's go.

Esquire is an independent, aggressive, private kind of individual. He has had one two-year lover relationship, and has done "things" from time to time, but hasn't the temperament to settle down with anyone. To provide a more stable social base than nightly tricks, Esquire has had a group of close gay friends he has known since his first years out, almost twenty-five years ago. The three men he shares the house with on Fire Island—one in advertising, one a banker, one who hasn't done much of anything since the inheritance—are a family of sorts. He also had his career. He became a partner of his firm in record time and did more than a creditable job. That was satisfying. He liked the people he worked with and the respect he commanded. Only one of his colleagues knew he was gay. The others, if they suspected, never mentioned it.

Esquire had never told his parents he was gay. Once at a large cocktail party in their home, his parents and a circle of friends were selling him on this beautiful, sensitive, wonderful girl he just had to meet—and in the midst of all the gracious adjectives that were being heaped on this young girl, whoever she was, Esquire asked loudly, "Sure, sure—but does she fuck?"

From then on, apparently, his mother was careful to skirt any issue, particularly in public, that might set off her all-too-healthy heterosexual son.

In sixteen years as a lawyer in New York Esquire maintained more than a comfortable standard of living, while contributing generously to his various alumni funds, causes, and campaigns (he is a director of one charity and a trustee of his old private school). He "retired" last year. In those sixteen years, with no life insurance bills to pay, no pediatricians, orthodontists, or gynecologists to pay, no Little Red School House tuition or Camp Winnipesaukee fee, Esquire had saved enough money to support himself modestly for the rest of his life. That had been his goal, to have the freedom to do anything he wanted, and now he has it. He plans to spend a couple of years going around the world, and then he will see what he feels like doing.

I might shoot for the same goal of financial independence and feel a special pleasure knowing I could quit work and go off at any time—but I'm not sure I would actually quit. It seems too risky to give up all your routines and most of your grounding and social relationships and strike out on your own, alone. I like to know where I'm going.

Yet isn't it fantastic? To have the self-made independence to fulfill one's potential? To be fully, or almost, master of your own fate? The anticipation of such a life may be more stimulating than the life itself. But such a future might be every bit as stimulating, I should think, as a traditional happy family life would be, two hours of commuting to the law firm each day until retirement at sixty-five.

Esquire took me to some of the bars and to the baths that

Charlie, the bashful model, was too conservative to frequent. Look at Esquire in his bell-bottom jeans, stoned on some $35 shit only New York attorneys can afford, dancing his head off with that lanky boy in the middle of the floor. This is the Tamburlaine, in the East Forties, a popular mixed dance bar, mostly gay, until it burned down, or was bombed some say, because it clashed with the quiet residential neighborhood. All types in this place. Esquire, who is flinging his NYAC-sun-room-tanned body in all directions in homage to the Rolling Stones tonight, will be earning $75 an hour tomorrow morning counseling IBM on the subtleties of antitrust precedents. His lanky friend came to New York from Dallas to earn $75 an hour modeling, when there is work. Right now there is none: Fresh faces are needed for the pages of the Sunday *Times* magazine—always fresh faces—so he settles for $1.05 an hour plus tips at Daly's. When you look like this lad and you work on New York's East Side, you get outrageous tips (some of the clientele can't resist), and tips are mostly "tax-free." Esquire might try to keep up with him and take him home tonight, but it would be a little awkward with me sleeping on the couch in the living room—and there is that meeting with the client at ten tomorrow. They will have dinner tomorrow night, instead.

Gay life in New York is so different from gay life in Boston. The bars are different. There are more of them, and they change faster. If you go to Sporters a couple of nights a week, you are bound to see many of your friends. If there is someone you want to meet, sooner or later a friend will introduce you, or you will find yourself standing next to him, both of you knowing that it is time to say hello because you both have been smiling a little the past few times you've seen each other there. There *are* some neighborhood bars in New York that have their regulars, but the game is played to a faster pace. With so many bars going at any time people hop around. In for a look—nobody here—out to another. And the bars go until four, so the crowded time extends much later—not from eleven to one on weekends as in Boston, but from eleven to two or three, seven days a week. What are the chances that you will ever see that man again who just passed by? What are the chances one of your friends knows him and can introduce you? The two of you may never bump into each other again. So you had better go up and say hello if you have any interest—and for his part, he had better not be too hard to get if he wants to be gotten.

So in New York, it is accepted practice for the guy standing next to you to stick out his hand, cold from the sweat of his beer bottle, and say "Hi. What's your name?"—sometimes even without telling you his first. You would never do that in Boston unless you had just come up from New York for the weekend and didn't know any better. Hell, if you didn't know any better, you might even be wearing your New York faggot Guccis and some kind of expensive shirt unbuttoned down to your solar plexus, exposing your New York faggot Puerto Rico tan. We are simpler folk in Boston, and more reserved.

Relationships tend to last longer in Boston than New York. In either city it takes a while to get on a last-name basis—getting to know you as you, not as a sex object that needs no name. But once you do, you are likely to stay in touch longer in Boston. There are fewer temptations to spin you dizzily on to other people, more barriers to loose living, more inhibitions, more conservatism.

Esquire took me to the Barn, which has since been closed down after someone's genitals were cut off with a switch-blade in the pitch-dark "back room," or so the story goes. The police are down on back rooms these days. How did Esquire ever *find* the Barn? It was in a warehouse district near the Village, where the streets have names instead of numbers and run randomly so as to confound all but the veteran cabbies and truck drivers. The building has no sign. There is no advertising, no number in the phone book. The area is completely deserted late at night, except for the people like us walking between the Village bars, so there are few people on the street to ask directions of. You go in a scarred unmarked metal door to a service elevator and wait for the huge car to come down. The elevator boy is unmistakable confirmation that this is the place, and when the door opens upstairs, you are in the midst of hundreds of people, drink-ing and dancing, on a gigantic, largely unpartitioned ware-house floor. What's the rest of the building used for? Who knows? Who is the landlord? It's not hard to guess. How did all these people find it? Word of mouth. It's "in." There's a back room, and the place is always jammed. Half the appeal is that it's so hard to find.

Christopher's End is (was?) at the end of Christopher Street and easier to find. They featured nude go-go boys and erotic slide shows on the wall. Uncle Edna's is a hus-tlers' bar up around the theater district. The Eagle's Nest is one of the leather bars way over by the piers on the lower West Side. Well, near the trucks. Do you want to go to the trucks? "Hi, Mom. I'd like you to meet my new friend, Raunch. I met him in one of the trailers on the waterfront." Is it possible that I am writing these things?

How about the Y, if you don't go in for trucks? The YMCA is like an international budget hotel chain for homosexuals. New York's West Side Y is the medallion in the chain. The Y is also a chain of budget health clubs for young married guys who still enjoy a good ball game to keep in shape, a shower, maybe a rubdown, and a little locker-room banter. Not all these jocks are as near ten on the scale as they would have you think, though they would surely flatten you to prove that they were. Just the way the Pope can excommunicate you to prove that abortion is evil.

If you would rather not stay at the Y when you come to New York, you could stay at the baths. The Continental is world-famous, though by no means the only gay baths in New York. Esquire goes to the Continental once a week, on average, and told me I should really come with him the next time I was in New York. I didn't like the image I had of older men with wrinkly paunches hanging over their towels, looking to see what was under my towel. I didn't like that at all. On the other hand, Golden Boy, too, was always selling me on the Continental—he loved to go to New York for a weekend and debauch a bit—and his description was appealing. Somehow I had pieced together a picture of a Holiday Inn kind of place, immaculate, where you could either rent a room (would the TV be color, I wondered?) or a locker and then swim, work out, sit in the sauna, dance, eat—a gay country club where you could smile at a fellow you liked and be in his room a minute later, doing it. I wasn't sure I could get into such impersonal sex, but it would still be fun to work out and swim and take a look, and you never know what kinds of Golden Boys might be walking around locker-room style at the baths. Wasn't this my high school locker-room fantasies come true? I could pretend the older men were the coaches, or alumni there for homecoming, and ignore them.

Eventually Esquire and I went. We walked into a small lobby—very small and un-Holiday-Inn-like. On the other side of a large glass window were two attendants—again, one look at the attendants and you know you are in the right place—and an entire wall of safe-deposit boxes. "Occupancy by More Than 900 Persons is Dangerous and Unlawful." Esquire and I both asked for rooms. He said I would feel more comfortable having a room to go back to in case I wanted to catch my breath by myself for a few minutes or, of course, if I found someone I wanted to make it with. The room was $10, which I was pleased to see you could charge on your Diners Club card—perhaps this place was like the Holiday Inn, after all. There were student rates, I noticed, too, hoping some students might have checked in that night.

We deposited our valuables in the safe-deposit boxes and were given keys to our rooms and towels. The keys are on wrist bands, so you can't lose them. The Continental baths are divided into three floors, and our "rooms" were on the third. Each room is barely large enough for a single bed and supplied with two clean sheets. There is a stool, a small mirror, a coat hook, and a yellow bulb with a string chain to switch it on and off. The ceiling is perhaps six and a half feet high, made of chicken wire. The real ceiling of the building is considerably higher. I presume the chicken wire is to keep things like underwear from being thrown around and to discourage people from climbing from one room to the next. The walls are thin plywood. There are speakers on this floor for the PA system—mainly calls to attendants to clean vacated rooms, or pages ("Will the BLBITW please come to the front desk?")—and no music. It's eerie. Dark except for some yellow and purple lights. Quiet except for the moans and slurps and sighs of sex. (GB tells me that is supposed to be erotic.) People talk quietly when they talk at all. Mainly, they stalk around the halls, which extend in all directions, mazelike, for what must be miles if you walked them all. Well, half a mile anyway, or close to it. Some of the room doors are open. If the yellow bulb is on, the occupant thinks your seeing him will encourage you to visit. If off, he thinks you will be more interested if it is left a little vague what you're getting into. If he is lying on his back, that means he wants one thing; on his stomach, another. It is proper etiquette for you, if you think you may have some commonality of interests, to walk in, take a closer look, and either stay or leave. All, perhaps, without saying a word. (Silence sometimes flatters these gentlemen, anyway.) I was too nearsighted to make any definite evaluations from outside the rooms in that fuzzy light and too embarrassed to venture inside for a reliable inspection. I knew most of these people had to be ugly when I saw them up close—what kind of guy was going to lie there in the first place? Certainly not me, for crying out loud—and I couldn't see having sex that way. I'm not good at sex, remember. I need someone who understands that, preferably someone who has an inhibition or two himself. How could I tell one of these pros the things I was not wild about doing, within earshot of, perhaps, 200 people. I could whisper, of course, or even just use hand signals—but how could I trust one of these strangers not to shout out, WHAT? *You mean you don't like to suck cock! My dear, are you gay or aren't you?* When I ran out of the room in embarrassment, I would have to wedge my way through the 200 curious queens who had gathered by the door.

None of this would happen, of course. It was just that, obviously, I was still not fully at ease with myself, to say the least. I still felt an unhealthy measure of superiority over these other people.

At any rate, most people walk around the baths in their towels, rather than lie in waiting. Those who only rent mini-lockers, gym lockers, or walk-in lockers (something for everybody), have no choice. They walk around the second or third floors, looking in open doors, or looking at others looking in open doors, or visiting The Dormitory, which sports a number of mattresses and a ten-watt light bulb, and is open to all. Thank you anyway.

I spent most of my time on the first floor, swimming in a small overheated pool with enough chlorine in it to kill any disease you can think of, or else watching Little Joe Cartwright on *Bonanza* in the color TV room, or else doing sit-ups and bench presses. I used the sun room, passed up a couple of invitations to dance, passed up the massage room, and couldn't buy anything at the snack bar because I had forgotten to take a dollar out of my wallet before putting it in the valuables box at the front desk.

Esquire led me around at first, explaining the "rules," but then disappeared with someone, and then with someone else, and then told me he was going home, he had an early client meeting in the morning. How many numbers had I had? Well, none. I was feeling sorry for myself. I couldn't get into it. Why was I so squeamish? What had there been about my toilet training that made that bad odor around the steam room so revolting?

As we were leaving, they announced a free buffet that

would start shortly by the pool; and next Saturday they would be featuring Bette Midler; and the free VD clinic would start in five minutes in Room 100. I might have stayed for a free athletes' foot clinic, but could have contracted nothing worse that evening. We left.

I went down to Norfolk to visit Freddie, my original crush, for a weekend. He lives at home in the summer and decided to have a talk with his parents when he saw that they had special-ordered *The Lord Won't Mind* from the local bookstore. In his case, the talk went well. Though his mother is convinced he is just going through a stage, she is happy so long as he is happy—and he is happy.

(Freddie's older brother is not so happy. He had married a girl, divorced her, married her again, had a child, and divorced her again. He was now unhappily married to a second girl. Did he honestly love these women until he had them, had to live with them, and then, almost despite himself, turn off? Was there some connection between whatever there had been about that family's life that had made Freddie gay and whatever had made his older brother unhappily married? If so, should society feel the same repulsion toward unhappily married straights as they do toward homosexuals?)

With Freddie I met Michael and Michael, who had not made the vain attempt to obtain a legal marriage certificate and a common last name (perhaps to avoid confusion), but who had been "married" for twenty-two years. No kids. Michael and Michael lived together in a beautiful Colonial home and were partners in a real estate firm. They were well liked in the community, whatever jokes may have been made behind their backs, and led pleasant, peaceful lives.

They attended concerts together, church together, parties together. They never went to the bar in Norfolk, but they entertained and visited their many gay friends. They were as faithful to each other as my parents are, even though it may have required more willpower at first.

In my limited experience, this kind of happy relationship is even rarer among gay people than among straight people. However, my sample is probably biased, because I make little effort to meet older gay people and I tend to go to bars and parties older gay lovers wouldn't be likely to go to. Perhaps more gay people "marry" and settle down for happy lives than I imagine. Certainly, Michael and Michael are not the only example I can think of. And as society becomes more tolerant, such relationships may become more commonplace.

I wonder whether Esquire could ever settle down this way, or whether I will. I am too aggressive and egotistical to live with someone who won't defer to my wishes and acknowledge, tacitly, my wicker-weave throne. I am competitive. But at the same time, I am too impatient to enjoy the company of someone who is not as aggressive as I am—and I am not stimulated by submissiveness. What is required is a fine balance, an equality, the kind of thing I think the feminists are after. Perhaps I will learn to share and live with another person, the experience with Chris notwithstanding. After all, I was emotionally about fifteen years old when I was going with Chris. Perhaps I simply am not ready to settle down, no different from many of my unmarried straight friends. After all, there is less social pressure for me to settle down with a gay guy than there is for my straight friends to marry (the understatement of the age?). And there is not the incentive to have kids at a reasonably early age so you don't die on them when they need you. Perhaps it is natural for gays to settle down later in life than straights.

Naturally, I am curious to know what I will be like in twenty or thirty years. And what of forty or fifty or even sixty years from now, should I live so long? When the real crunch comes. Offhand I can't think of any really old gay people I have met, at least not in an explicitly gay situation where I could hear about that side of their life.

Surely forty years from now the world will be unlike anything we know now, if it is here at all. Is there any sense in speculating that far into the future? For the moment it is sufficient for me that I intend to provide for a comfortable old age. And that god-damned Chris had just better stay around to clear his god-damned throat in that annoying way from the next wheelchair over in Sunny Faggots' Rest Home.

CHAPTER 15

Tomorrow the movers come to take my stuff to Washington. I wouldn't have minded moving myself in a U-Haul, but with IBM selling at $400 a share, we don't do things that way. Monday I start work again. Frankly, I've missed the discipline. For the past six weeks I've been sleeping late, working at the kitchen table in my not-too-clean cutoffs, crumbs on the floor, dishes piled in the sink—no one around to make me feel important or needed, no one for me to need or take to lunch, no one to argue with. I think I'll just leave the sink the way it is and buy a new set of kitchenware in Washington. The bottom layer of dishes has probably been there for close to two months now, and I might not be able to get them clean even if I could bring myself to try. The only thing I hate more than setting the table is doing the dishes.

There is not time to play out the Peyton Place romances I could tell you about. How I fell for an impossibly unattainable model named Randy who turned out to be both attainable and an impossible bore; how when Randy was unattainable, it was because he was busy falling for Golden Boy, who was still too hung up on Dennis Moyer to take

any notice—while Dennis himself had chanced to run into
Hunter, Chris's new lover, while Chris was away; how
Dennis fell for Hunter (and subsequently for Chris, and
subsequently for your humble narrator); how Hunter was
beginning to feel that leaving Craig, his lover of the past
four years, for Chris may not have been such a good idea after all and in the meantime was quoted as saying to Golden
Boy: "I wonder what would have happened if I had met you
before I met Chris?"; how a GB-Hunter fling was not forth-
coming both because GB remembered the consequences of
his last fling with one of Chris's lovers (your humble narrator, again) and also because it was about that time that word
filtered back to GB of Hunter's thing with Dennis, which
naturally drove GB up his own patented Wailing Wall; or
how they all lived happily ever after.

I don't expect you to remember that for Tuesday's quiz;
but I have read it over, and it is accurate—even if it leaves
out a few characters along the way. The "they all lived happily ever after" part I just threw in to try to regain control
of the sentence. Whether that part is accurate remains to be
seen. Give it a military background and you might turn that
one incestuous sentence into a gay *War and Peace*. You
might, that is, if you were a novelist. But even if I were a
novelist, I'm not sure there is anything awfully "novel" in
what we were doing. Isn't this what many kids were doing in
the tenth grade? Billy and Janey just broke up because Janey
told Mike she would go to the dance with him. But when
Herbie heard what Mike had done to his best friend Billy,
Herbie tackled Mike extra hard in the scrimmage and broke
Mike's ankle. Now Mike can't take Janey to the dance, but
now Billy won't take her either: Billy doesn't ever want to

have anything to do with Janey and is in the depths of despair, but is taking little Mary Ann out behind the greenhouse, anyway, just to keep in practice.

The difference between the movies *Bob and Carol and Ted and Alice* and *Bob and Daryl and Ted and Alex*, besides the difference in their Motion Pictures Guild ratings, is that more combinations and permutations of relationships are likely to occur in the latter. The mathematical sign for permutations is "!". I begin to understand why when I think of Chris and GB and Hunter and Dennis and me!

I don't mean to make light of all the "intrigue" and emotion of the last two years. At times I was entirely caught up in it. Certainly, whenever I knew GB and Chris were together without me, I felt left out and, despite myself, jealous. But even if I had time to detail all our comings and goings, I am sure it would be of interest only to our little group.

Now the group is being broken up geographically. Chris was graduated from Harvard Business School in June and has left for a management training program with his new employer in Atlanta. I am going to Washington, $38 from Atlanta by Eastern night coach and 20 cents a minute by phone.

Golden Boy won a Rotary fellowship to study for a year at the London School of Economics and will be leaving shortly for England, if he can tear himself away from one of the pro football players I've alluded to. Golden Boy finally got over Dennis Moyer, at least partially, with the rationalization that he was too good for Dennis and that Dennis wasn't even perceptive enough to realize it. Dennis will be in Boston next year, and for the indefinite future, with his law firm.

Hunter is back with his pre-Chris lover, Craig, perhaps for another four years or another forty. Probably for another four months. But that unkind prediction just reflects my innate hostility toward Hunter for having diverted some of Chris's attention from me to himself and for having hurt Chris. Randy, who wasn't really part of our group, but who found himself in my *War and Peace* paragraph anyway, is looking for modeling jobs in New York. His last job was an Army recruiting ad. You know: Join the Action Army and be a real man like me.

Parker Martinson, Mr. Paranoia, came over yesterday to say good-bye. I will miss our daily telephone conversations. My daily therapy for him was at least as much therapy for me: There is perhaps no better way to make someone conscious of his own good fortune—to make him happy—than to give him the task of cheering up someone else.

Parker's "problem" is that he is about five on my scale from one to ten. I think being five has the most potential for pleasure and the most for pain. If you can master and feel comfortable with bisexuality, you can love everyone and have everyone love you. You can see beauty in twice as many faces; you can live a richer, fuller life. If, like Parker, you can't master it, it can bug you no end. Parker won't allow himself to enjoy guys; his sexual appetite for guys distracts him from enjoying girls. He has built "his problem" into a veritable institution in his mind, even if he does take some consolation from his cosmic miserableness, as I used to.

Relax, Parker. Tell Hank, Parker. Tell everyone. Enjoy it. You can't possibly be happy if you hate yourself, if you don't like the image you have of yourself. I think happiness is being satisfied with what you are. Shock treatments aren't going to change you, Parker. You are always going to like guys as well as girls. It will be easier for you to change your opinion of yourself than for you to change your fundamental sexual orientation. You should be proud and delighted that you have the best of both worlds.

Just the other day, Parker, I was asking Chris whether if science came up with a pill to make gays straight, he would take it. He asked, "Could I still like boys?" You see? To him the best deal would be the deal *you* have: to be able to make it with chicks the way you do, to have sex with them, to have dinner with them, to marry them and have a family with them, the way you will—but to like boys, too. I envy you, too, Parker. I wish I liked girls, too. Maybe I wish it only in an abstract way, since the whole thought really kind of turns me off; but it's still a nice idea in theory.

"Would *you* take that pill and make yourself straight?" Parker asked me. No, I wouldn't. That would make me an entirely different person. *That would be like killing myself.* I have learned to love my array of quaint fuck-ups. That's the trick, Parker: If you just make up your mind to like yourself, you will be happy. Once happy, you will have all the more reason to like yourself. It's as much a self-fulfilling prophecy as anything else: To like yourself, you have to think you're nifty. To be nifty, you have to be happy. To be happy, you have to like yourself. To like yourself, you have to think you're nifty. To be nifty, you have to be happy. To be happy, you have to like—

"That's the most ridiculous thing I've ever heard," said Parker.

I know. It's very much like a religion: I define myself as happy. I take it on faith. It may sound irrational, this defining myself as happy—but what religion *is* rational? What rational purpose *is* there for living? What rationality underlies society's prejudice against homosexuals? Hmmmm, Parker?

"Well, that may work out for you, but whatever you do, don't you ever tell anyone about *me*. Promise me that."

"Okay, Parker, I promise. Don't forget to visit me. I hear 'the bushes' in Washington are out of sight."

I haven't managed to say all I wanted to or to say it properly or in a way that would inspire the indignation I wanted you to feel. Throughout the book I have felt like adding footnoted apologies to gay readers for sounding simpleminded, naïve, and supercilious. It should go without saying that having tried so hard for years to remain ignorant of it and having been out a relatively short time, I don't know that much about homosexuality. I only know what it was like for me to come to terms—or to begin to, anyway—with my own.

Dr. David Reuben, on the other hand, purports to know a great deal about homosexuality. Indeed, Dr. David Reuben, a psychiatrist, claims to know *Everything You Always Wanted to Know About Sex but Were Afraid to Ask*. Since his book has sold some 8,000,000 copies to date, it is likely that his chapter on homosexuality has been more widely read than any other.

Dr. Reuben explains that homosexual encounters are generally impersonal. A guy goes down to a bowling alley, sits on a toilet in the men's room, plays footsie with the guy in the next stall. They exchange notes on pieces of toilet paper, then suck each other's penises, then leave. "No feeling, no sentiment, no nothing," explains Dr. Reuben. "*Are all homosexual contacts as impersonal as that?* No. Most are much more impersonal." Dr. Reuben explains that most of us don't even have time to write notes or even to close the bathroom stall door for a measure of privacy. "A masturbation machine might do it better," he explains. "*But* all *homosexuals aren't like that, are they*? Unfortunately, they are just like that," he says.

Last night I went down to Sporters to say good-bye to some friends. The only notable occurrence was my meeting an Air Force sergeant who was passing through Boston. He was originally from Albuquerque, New Mexico. He had been engaged to be married for three years, but kept putting off the marriage. Last year he broke off the engagement and came out. Aged twenty-six. *Aged twenty-six.* I wonder how many people there are on the earth, this instant, who are ostensibly straight, but who have this terrible shameful secret gnawing out their insides, making them miserable. How many are there like that—aged eleven? Sixteen? Twenty-two? Twenty-six? Thirty-four? Forty-seven? Eighty-three?

CHAPTER 16

I told them. They said that so far as they were concerned, I was still the best little boy in the world.

AFTERWORD

I was twenty-five when the foregoing was written; I am twenty-nine now. Look how the world has changed—and not changed. Imagine: a six-part series on the sports pages of newspapers around the country about pro athletes who are gay; a front-page *Wall Street Journal* story about *The Advocate* (whose own circulation has doubled in the past year); a lead piece in *The Sunday New York Times* travel section on an all-gay cruise; a *Time* cover story on a much-decorated gay Army sergeant. Doubtless, a lot of eyes have been opened to "the silent minority." Paul Newman, in *The Front Runner*, if that film ever gets made, could open a lot more.

But not that much has changed. At a party in Beverly Hills recently, "Adam Smith," author of *The Money Game* and *Powers of Mind*, confided with disdain: "This is really fag city!" It was even worse than he thought, I told him—I was gay, too. Would he have called it "nigger city" if there had been a lot of blacks at the party? He said he saw my point—but I doubt he changed his mind. A week or two later, the Supreme Court (not mine, the real one) refused even to *consider* overturning state laws which ban consenting adults from doing what they want behind closed doors. And in Italy, a seventeen-year-old hustler was becoming a national hero for having brutally murdered filmmaker Pier Paolo Pasolini. The hustler had willingly drilled Pasolini for thirty dollars and a ride in his Alfa Romeo; but when Pasolini wanted to reverse positions, the hustler killed him. His father exuded a sort of confused pride when interviewed on Italian TV, hoping that in a similar situation he would have acted with equal courage.

I have changed and not changed, also. I am no longer lost in the Pyrenees (if the road to good sex runs from Lisbon to Leningrad, as postulated earlier); I am slogging through snowdrifts in the Italian Alps. Substantially further along, in other words, but still a little off course. I have not let my gayness control my life, which I think is important. But neither have I come fully to terms with it nor managed to set up the kind of loving long-term relationship I think I want.

I came close. To my astonishment, I found myself unrestrainedly in love with someone—a dentist, not a cowboy— who was also unrestrainedly in love with me. At the same time, no less! I was never happier than the nearly a year we were lovers—nor unhappier than the nearly a year it has taken me to adjust, more or less, to being best friends instead. Having seen how good it can be, I'll admit life seems much emptier without it.

Chris, meanwhile, remains a close friend, as do Parker Martinson and Golden Boy. Chris has been with a new friend for two years now and is doing well professionally. Golden Boy has been with his new lover nearly *four* years, more power to him, and is himself an up-and-coming executive. Parker Martinson, Mr. Paranoia, is as neurotic as ever, but coming into his own.

In reading my own book, four years later, I naturally found quite a bit that made me uncomfortable. I have made two kinds of changes from the original: first, minor changes of English to make it read better or clearer; second, cuts, particularly in the second half, to make it read faster. Having heard from four million people that they liked the first half but that the second half dragged, I began to get the feeling that maybe the second half did drag. So I made a few cuts—and probably should have made more.

One change I would have liked to make but didn't was the pen name. Besides spoiling the book for many a gay activist, the pen name is slightly ludicrous since just about everyone who knows me knows who John Reid is. But it still comes down to the same thing: Would the pain and embarrassment using my own name would cause my parents be worth whatever good it would do? If I were Joe Namath or Johnny Carson or someone, there would be more of a point to it. As it is, it would be the wrong thing to do. For now, anyway.

John Reid
August 1, 1976

AFTERWORD—1993

I'm fine. A lot of my friends are not. I think it's time to write another book. I never seem to get around to it, but maybe now I will.